ACOUSTIC
GUITAR
PRIVATE LESSONS

RHYTHM GUITAR ESSENTIALS

string
letter
media

Publisher: David A. Lusterman

Group Publisher and Editorial Director: Dan Gabel

Editor: Jeffrey Pepper Rodgers

Music Editor and Engraver: Andrew DuBrock

Art Director: Barbara Summer

Production Designer: Kristin Wallace

ISBN 978-1-4234-6414-3

This book was produced by String Letter Publishing, Inc.

501 Canal Blvd, Suite J, Richmond, CA 94804

(510) 215-0010; stringletter.com

AUDIO

The complete set of audio downloads for the musical examples and songs in *Rhythm Guitar Essentials* is available for free at **store.acousticguitar.com/RGE**.

CONTENTS

INTRODUCTION

Rhythm rules. Sure, lead guitar is cool—who doesn't dream of wowing the crowd with a spectacular solo? But without great rhythm, lead guitar heroism and pyrotechnics don't mean a thing. The rhythm is what gets listeners' heads bobbing and their feet tapping, and what makes them truly *feel* the music. In bands of all stripes, from blues to bluegrass to rock, the rhythm guitarist plays an essential role in bringing grooves to life. And if you're playing solo, of course, you are your own band—so it's extra important to build a solid foundation of rhythm.

This 12-pack of lessons from the master teachers at *Acoustic Guitar* magazine offers all sorts of tools for your rhythm guitar kit, from fundamental grooves used in folk, rock, soul, and country through creative and open-ended ways to expand your rhythmic vocabulary. Along the way you'll hone the technique of both the strumming/picking hand that drives the rhythm, and the fretting hand that creates the chords. You'll learn how to add colors to your rhythm parts *and* how to simplify them for a stark and powerful sound.

The aim of these lessons is to provide you with rhythm ideas that you can apply to whatever kind of music you play, instrumental or vocal, pick or fingerstyle, solo or with a band. Happy exploring.

—*Jeffrey Pepper Rodgers*

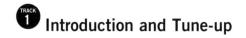 **Introduction and Tune-up**

MUSIC NOTATION KEY

The music in this book is written in standard notation and tablature. Here's how to read it.

STANDARD NOTATION

Standard notation is written on a five-line staff. Notes are written in alphabetical order from A to G.

The duration of a note is determined by three things: the note head, stem, and flag. A whole note (𝅝) equals four beats. A half note (𝅗𝅥) is half of that: two beats. A quarter note (𝅘𝅥) equals one beat, an eighth note (𝅘𝅥𝅮) equals half of one beat, and a 16th note (𝅘𝅥𝅯) is a quarter beat (there are four 16th notes per beat).

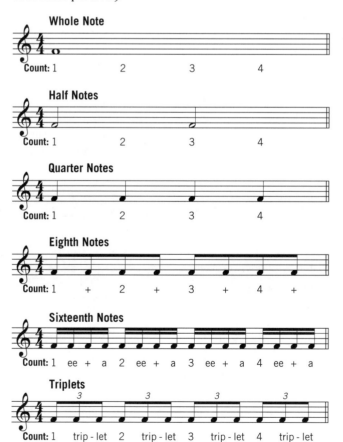

The fraction (4/4, 3/4, 6/8, etc.) or 𝄴 character shown at the beginning of a piece of music denotes the time signature. The top number tells you how many beats are in each measure, and the bottom number indicates the rhythmic value of each beat (4 equals a quarter note, 8 equals an eighth note, 16 equals a 16th note, and 2 equals a half note). The most common time signature is 4/4, which signifies four quarter notes per measure and is sometimes designated with the symbol 𝄴 (for common time). The symbol 𝄵 stands for cut time (2/2). Most songs are either in 4/4 or 3/4.

TABLATURE

In tablature, the six horizontal lines represent the six strings of the guitar, with the first string on the top and sixth on the bottom. The numbers refer to fret numbers on a given string. The notation and tablature in this book are designed to be used in tandem—refer to the notation to get the rhythmic information and note durations, and refer to the tablature to get the exact locations of the notes on the guitar fingerboard.

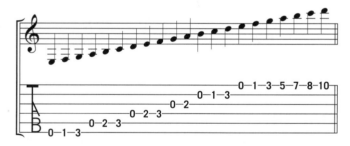

FINGERINGS

Fingerings are indicated with small numbers and letters in the notation. Fretting-hand fingering is indicated with 1 for the index finger, 2 the middle, 3 the ring, 4 the pinky, and *T* the thumb. Picking-hand fingering is indicated by *i* for the index finger, *m* the middle, *a* the ring, *c* the pinky, and *p* the thumb. Circled numbers indicate the string the note is played on. Remember that the fingerings indicated are only suggestions;

PICK AND STRUM DIRECTION

In music played with a flatpick, downstrokes (toward the floor) and upstrokes (toward the ceiling) are shown as follows. Slashes in the notation and tablature indicate a strum through the previously played chord.

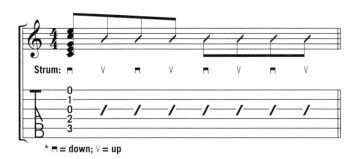

* ⊓ = down; V = up

CHORD DIAGRAMS

Chord diagrams show where the fingers go on the fingerboard. Frets are shown horizontally. The thick top line represents the nut. A Roman numeral to the right of a diagram indicates a chord played higher up the neck (in this case the top horizontal line is thin). Strings are shown as vertical lines. The line on the far left represents the sixth (lowest) string, and the line on the far right represents the first (highest) string. Dots show where the fingers go, and thick horizontal lines indicate barres. Numbers above the diagram are left-hand finger numbers, as used in standard notation. Again, the fingerings are only suggestions. An X indicates a string that should be muted or not played; 0 indicates an open string.

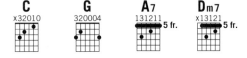

CAPOS

If a capo is used, a Roman numeral indicates the fret where the capo should be placed. The standard notation and tablature is written as if the capo were the nut of the guitar. For instance, a tune capoed anywhere up the neck and played using key-of-G chord shapes and fingerings will be written in the key of G. Likewise, open strings held down by the capo are written as open strings.

TUNINGS

Alternate guitar tunings are given from the lowest (sixth) string to the highest (first) string. For instance, D A D G B E indicates standard tuning with the bottom string dropped to D. Standard notation for songs in alternate tunings always reflects the actual pitches of the notes. Arrows underneath tuning notes indicate strings that are altered from standard tuning and whether they are tuned up or down.

VOCAL TUNES

Vocal tunes are sometimes written with a fully tabbed-out introduction and a vocal melody with chord diagrams for the rest of the piece. The tab intro is usually your indication of which strum or fingerpicking pattern to use in the rest of the piece. The melody with lyrics underneath is the melody sung by the vocalist. Occasionally, smaller notes are written with the melody to indicate the harmony part sung by another vocalist. These are not to be confused with cue notes, which are small notes that indicate melodies that vary when a section is repeated. Listen to a recording of the piece to get a feel for the guitar accompaniment and to hear the singing if you aren't skilled at reading vocal melodies.

ARTICULATIONS

There are a number of ways you can articulate a note on the guitar. Notes connected with slurs (not to be confused with ties) in the tablature or standard notation are articulated with either a hammer-on, pull-off, or slide. Lower notes slurred to higher notes are played as hammer-ons; higher notes slurred to lower notes are played as pull-offs. While it's usually obvious that slurred notes are played as hammer-ons or pull-offs, an *H* or *P* is included above the tablature as an extra reminder.

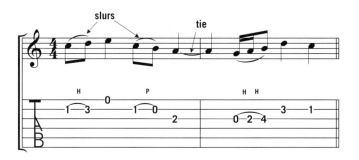

Slides are represented with a dash, and an S is included above the tab. A dash preceding a note represents a slide into the note from an indefinite point in the direction of the slide; a dash following a note indicates a slide off of the note to an indefinite point in the direction of the slide. For two slurred notes connected with a slide, you should pick the first note and then slide into the second.

Bends are represented with upward curves, as shown in the next example. Most bends have a specific destination pitch—the number above the bend symbol shows how much the bend raises the string's pitch: ¼ for a slight bend, ½ for a half step, 1 for a whole step.

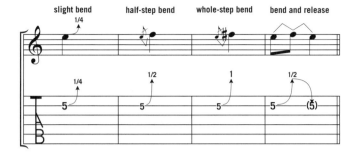

Grace notes are represented by small notes with a dash through the stem in standard notation and with small numbers in the tab. A grace note is a very quick ornament leading into a note, most commonly executed as a hammer-on, pull-off, or slide. In the first example below, pluck the note at the fifth fret on the beat, then quickly hammer onto the seventh fret. The second example is executed as a quick pull-off from the second fret to the open string. In the third example, both notes at the fifth fret are played simultaneously (even though it appears that the fifth fret, fourth string, is to be played by itself), then the seventh fret, fourth string, is quickly hammered.

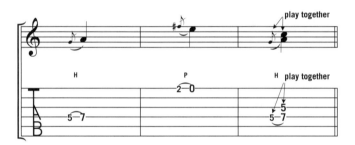

HARMONICS

Harmonics are represented by diamond-shaped notes in the standard notation and a small dot next to the tablature numbers. Natural harmonics are indicated with the text "Harmonics" or "Harm." above the tablature. Harmonics articulated with the right hand (often called artificial harmonics) include the text "R.H. Harmonics" or "R.H. Harm." above the tab. Right-hand harmonics are executed by lightly touching the harmonic node (usually 12 frets above the open string or fretted note) with the right-hand index finger and plucking the string with the thumb or ring finger or pick. For extended phrases played with right-hand harmonics, the fretted notes are shown in the tab along with instructions to touch the harmonics 12 frets above the notes.

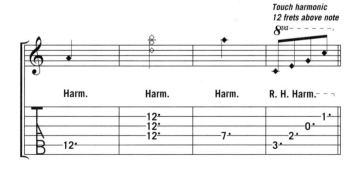

REPEATS

One of the most confusing parts of a musical score can be the navigation symbols, such as repeats, *D.S. al Coda*, *D.C. al Fine*, *To Coda*, etc. Repeat symbols are placed at the beginning and end of the passage to be repeated.

You should ignore repeat symbols with the dots on the right side the first time you encounter them; when you come to a repeat symbol with dots on the left side, jump back to the previous repeat symbol facing the opposite direction (if there is no previous symbol, go to the beginning of the piece). The next time you come to the repeat symbol, ignore it and keep going unless it includes instructions such as "Repeat three times."

A section will often have a different ending after each repeat. The example below includes a first and a second ending. Play until you hit the repeat symbol, jump back to the previous repeat symbol and play until you reach the bracketed first ending, skip the measures under the bracket and jump immediately to the second ending, and then continue.

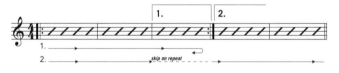

D.S. stands for *dal segno* or "from the sign." When you encounter this indication, jump immediately to the sign (𝄋). *D.S.* is usually accompanied by *al Fine* or *al Coda*. Fine indicates the end of a piece. A coda is a final passage near the end of a piece and is indicated with ⊕. *D.S. al Coda* simply tells you to jump back to the sign and continue on until you are instructed to jump to the coda, indicated with *To Coda* ⊕.

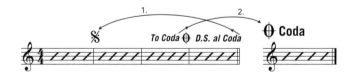

D.C. stands for *da capo* or "from the beginning." Jump to the top of the piece when you encounter this indication.

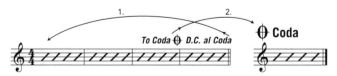

D.C. al Fine tells you to jump to the beginning of a tune and continue until you encounter the *Fine* indicating the end of the piece (ignore the *Fine* the first time through).

NINE CLASSIC GROOVES

Chris Grampp

Imagine you're playing guitar with friends around a camp-fire, rockin' out in a Beatles sing-along at a party, or learn-ing your favorite oldies off the radio. You will likely encounter many musical styles, and this lesson will give you the rhythmic vocabulary to help you play along with some of those songs. We'll cover some of the basics of folk, country, rock 'n' roll, soul, and pop.

Rhythm guitar begins with solid left- and right-hand tech-nique. When fingering a chord with your left hand, you can think of the chord as either "on," in which the notes ring, or "off," where your fingers are still in place but are lightly touch-ing the strings, deadening the sound. Begin each strum by sending your right forearm down (or up for upstrokes) in a broad arc beginning an inch or two before the sixth string and ending an inch or two after the first string. Snap your wrist in the direction of the strum just as your hand strikes the strings, as if you're flicking water off your fist.

Most of the examples in this lesson are shown with closed chords (no open strings). Try to play them as written and keep the notes from ringing past their written duration. I also recommend that you use a pick, medium gauge or heavier, to maximize the percussiveness of your strum. If you're having trouble with any of these rhythms, try practicing them with a metronome set to a slow tempo and gradually increase your speed as you get more comfortable.

> *Snap your wrist in the direction of the strum just as your hand strikes the strings, as if you're flicking water off your fist.*

Boom-Chuck

The boom-chuck beat is one of the first rhythms guitarists learn, and for good reason: you can play thousands of folk and country songs in this style. **Example 1** begins with a bass note on the root of the C chord (the "boom") followed by the rest of the chord (the "chuck"). The second bass note is a G (the fifth of the C chord) and is again followed by the rest of the chord. This figure, called an alternating bass, tends to sound better if the fifth is played below the root rather than above it, but cer-tain chord voicings won't allow you to do this. It's usually best to play the "booms" and "chucks" with downstrokes. When

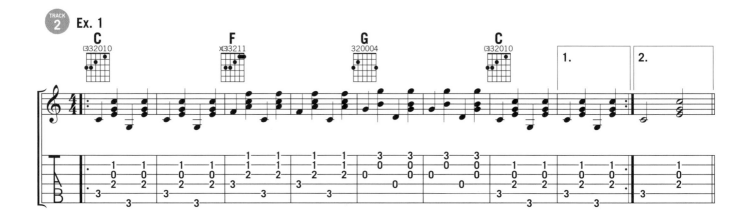

playing at faster tempos, try making the "chuck" staccato (rapid, brief, and clipped in sound) by lifting your fingers off the chord just after you play it. At slower tempos let it ring.

Example 2 substitutes a bass run for a strum in each measure preceding a new chord. Bass runs are a series of notes that lead into the root of the next chord. The notes can be chord tones (notes in the chord) or passing tones (notes in between chord tones).

Example 3 adds an upstroke strum to the first "chuck" of the measure, changing it from a quarter-note chord to two eighth-note chords. The rhythm is livelier and works well over

faster tempos. Good boom-chuck songs (there are too many to count) include "Your Cheatin' Heart," "Long Black Veil," and "Oh Lonesome Me."

Hootenanny Beat

The hootenanny beat (**Example 4**) is an all-out strumming fiesta. The first measure alternates quarter- and eighth-note chords, giving the rhythm a syncopated, swinging feel before ending on a quarter-note chord. The second measure begins like the first but ends with a flourish of three eighth-note

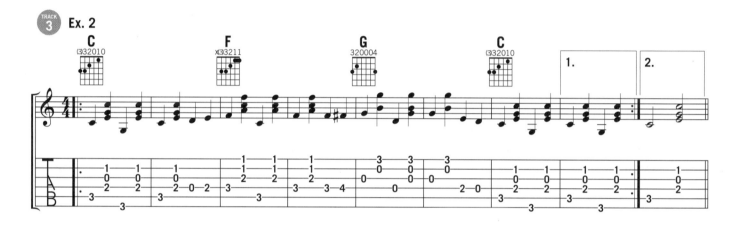

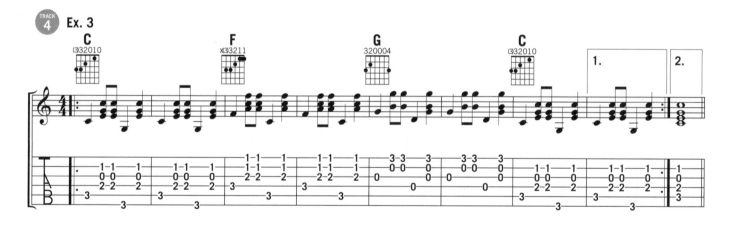

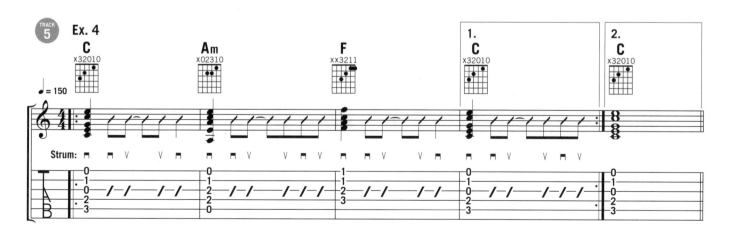

chords for contrast. Strum this beat heartily over "Someday Soon," "Don't Think Twice, It's All Right," and "Where Have All the Flowers Gone." It also works over doo-wop and rock songs from the 1950s and '60s like "Little Darlin'" and "Travelin' Man."

Speaking of rock 'n' roll, let's move on now to five classic rock beats.

Wall of Eighths

This rhythm (**Example 5**) consists of a single chord played eight times per measure (counted one-and two-and three-and four-and), with the beats (one, two, three, four) played with downstrokes, and the offbeats (the *ands*) with upstrokes. The wall of eighths also makes a great strumming exercise. Keep your right hand alternating evenly up and down eight times per measure. You may notice differences in attack, tone, volume, and timing between your down- and upstrokes, since you use different muscles to create them. Try to make both strokes sound as similar as possible and keep your timing even.

Each measure contains one chord, but when you play it, alternate between the bottom half (beats one and three) and the top half (beats two and four). The dot under each chord means it is to be played staccato to maintain rhythmic separa-

tion; as soon as you strum it, turn it "off" by loosening your fingers to clip the sound.

To intensify the groove, try slapping the strings lightly with your right-hand fingers on beats two and four as you strum. The second and fourth beats are known as the backbeats and cause the music to sway back and forth when accented. It takes practice to slap the strings without muffling the chord, but it's well worth the effort, especially when you're playing without a percussionist.

You can use the wall-of-eighths rhythm on classic rock songs such as "Roll Over Beethoven," "Nadine," and "Woolly Bully." If you mute the strings and play all the notes as downstrokes, you'll produce a sound that goes with 1980s pop tunes such as "Time After Time," "I Touch Myself," and "Every Breath You Take." To mute the strings, place the heel of your right hand lightly on top of the strings just in front of the bridge. Then strum with your wrist while keeping your hand on the strings.

Soul Beat

This soul rhythm (**Example 6**) begins with a two-note dyad that sets up the fuller chords that follow. I often "ghost," or lightly strum, the dyad rather then playing it at full volume. The second chord lands on the backbeat and is followed by a

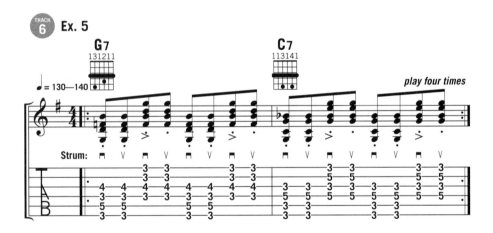

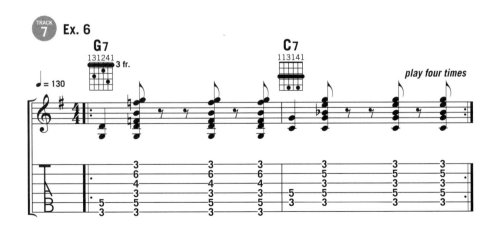

RHYTHM GUITAR ESSENTIALS

syncopation on the *and* of beat three. Syncopation, the accenting of weaker upbeats, creates rhythmic anticipation by placing the chord just before where you expect to hear it. Keep your right hand moving up and down at all times, and strike the strings lightly with your pick during the rests to keep the groove intact. (Don't overdo it, however; too much string noise can create clutter.) Try using this rhythm on soul hits like "In the Midnight Hour" and "Take Me to the River."

Bop Shoo-Bop

This two-measure rhythm (**Example 7**), drawn from the vocal backup in the Beatles' tune "Boys," resembles the soul beat but contains an additional chord just before the syncopation on beat six. The top notes of these two chords (which fall over the "shoo-bop") alternate between the root (G) and the domi-

nant seventh (F♮) to create a feeling of swing. The second measure begins with a full chord rather than a dyad and has no pickup chord at the end. Think "bop-bop shoo-bop" as you play this measure. Try this rhythm over "What'd I Say," "Rockin' Robin," and "Boys."

"La Bamba" Beat

In this popular 1960s rhythm (**Example 8**), the final chord of the first measure is tied to the first chord of the next measure. As a result the two measures flow together, complementing the cyclical chord progression shown in the example. You can also play a snappier version of this rhythm (bars 3–4), in which the quarter-note chords become eighth notes followed by rests. Try playing this beat over "La Bamba," "Get Off of My Cloud," "Good Lovin'," and "Twist and Shout."

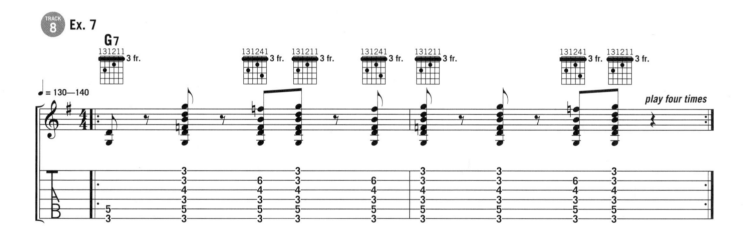

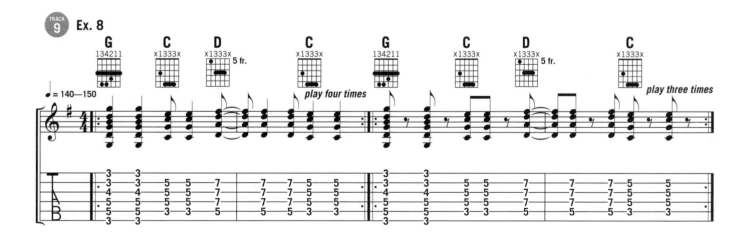

Summer of Love Vamp

This variation (**Example 9**) begins with a lively dotted-eighth/16th/eighth combination followed by a quarter-note rest for breathing room. You can hear this figure on the chorus to "Funkytown" from the *Shrek 2* soundtrack. The second half of the measure answers the first with a downstroke chord on the *and* of beat three, followed by two rapid 16th notes.

The dotted-eighth and 16th-note chords make this rhythm a little more difficult to count than the previous ones. Begin by dividing each measure into 16 beats. The first strum falls over beats one, two, and three; the next on beat four; and the third on beats five and six. Rest for beats seven through ten, then strum for beats 11 and 12, again on 13, and again on 14. Rest for beats 15 and 16. To add a little spice, insert a 16th-note chord in front of the dotted-eighth chord in the second half of the measure (bars 3 and 4).

This groove works well behind lead guitar solos played over medium tempos. You can hear the Grateful Dead use it on the DVD *Festival Express*. Try it over "Knock on Wood" and "Ode to Billie Joe."

Each rhythm in this lesson will vary depending on the tempo, the characteristics of the song you're playing, and your musical sense. Listen to the audio tracks to hear my interpretations, and then take some time to develop your own feeling for each style. Most importantly, listen carefully to recordings of your favorite artists and figure out the rhythm guitar parts on a song-by-song basis. Once you get tuned into a wide variety of accompaniment styles, you'll really appreciate how much a strong rhythm contributes to a song, and you'll be on your way to building a large repertoire of backup techniques.

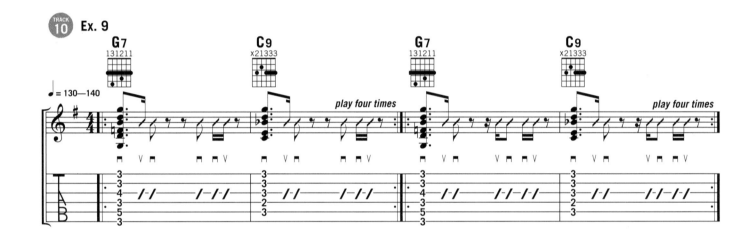

TRACK 10 **Ex. 9**

RHYTHM GUITAR ESSENTIALS

CONNECT YOUR CHORDS

Karen Hogg

After you've mastered basic open chords, you'll realize that there is more to rhythm guitar than meets the ear. Have you ever listened to a song and realized that, despite having only three or four chords, it doesn't sound simple? Great guitarists in every style of music, from Norman Blake to Jimi Hendrix, know that even the simplest songs can become more interesting by using melodic ideas and bass lines to connect chords. This lesson will focus on a few of these ideas—bass runs, sus chords, and riffs—to help your rhythm playing come alive.

Bring On the Bass

One of the key tricks guitarists use to spice up simple songs is creating bass lines between strums to lead the ear from one chord to the next. **Example 1** shows an easy, repeating pattern that moves back and forth between open-position G and C chords. The bass line in measure 2 climbs from a G note (on beat one) to A and B notes on beats three and four, creating a sense of movement by leading your ear to the C chord. The B and A notes at the end of measure 4 lead back to the G chord. When creating bass lines, be careful about where you place them rhythmically. You want to lead the ear to the next chord, but you have to make sure you get there at the right time. In Example 1, the bass line going to the C chord arrives at the C note just in time for the downbeat of measure 3.

As you can tell by listening to any good bass player, there are many ways to construct bass lines. **Example 2** shows one of the most common: a line that moves from the root to the

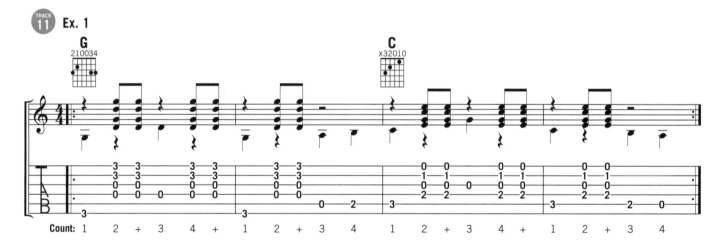

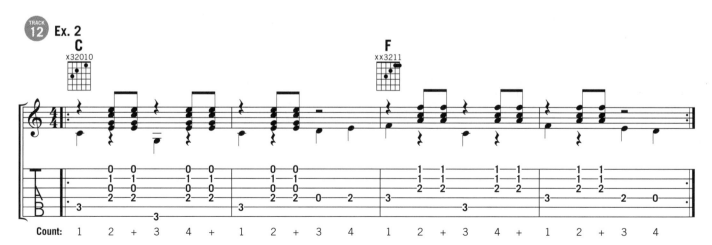

fifth of the chord—the same fret on the next lower string down (on the third beat of measures 1 and 3). Lines like this appear often in bluegrass, country, and other rootsy styles.

For even more country flavor, try the lick in **Example 3**, which travels from an E chord to a B7. For the last note in measure 4, use your middle finger to fret the F♯ on the second fret of the low E string. But before you hit the note, lightly pull the string downward (toward the floor) with your fretting finger, so that when you pluck it, it sounds more like a G. Keeping your finger on the note, let it pull you back to F♯. This is called bending the note. This bend, which sounds a lot like the bass riff from Johnny Cash's "Folsom Prison Blues," is a cool way to get back to the E chord.

All of these examples deal with open-position chords, but it's a good idea to practice bass lines up the neck with barre chords as well. Any of the bass lines you use with open strings can also be played in closed position. **Example 4** demonstrates a few bass runs between B♭, F, and E♭ barre chords. Notice the chromatic line between the F and E♭ chords in measure 2.

Get Yourself Suspended

Many guitarists use suspended chords (sus chords, for short) to fill time between chord changes, particularly when a song stays on one chord for a long time. Suspended chords are slight alterations of major chords, and there are two types: sus2 and sus4. In a sus2 chord, one of the chord tones—the third—is dropped a whole step (two frets). In a sus4 chord, the third is raised a half step—a single fret.

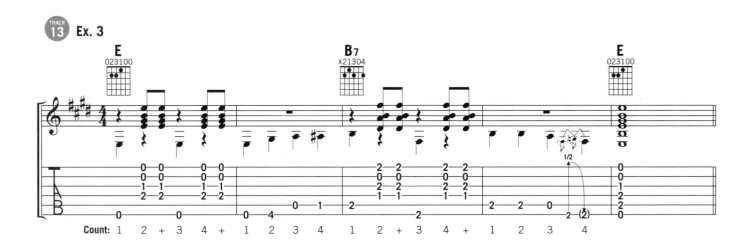

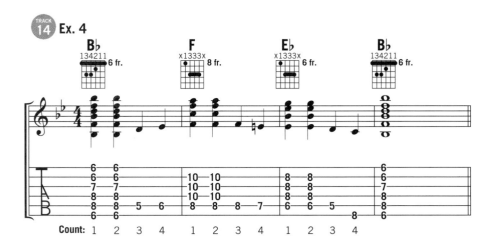

    RHYTHM GUITAR ESSENTIALS

Try **Example 5**, which adds suspensions to a basic D–A progression. Once you've played through the example a few times, try playing just the D and A chords with the same rhythm, but without the suspensions. Both versions will sound fine, but the version with the sus chords should sound a little richer.

Riff It Up!

Adding short riffs between chords can often make things more interesting, particularly between verses of a song, or when there is no other melody to draw listeners' attention. You can create a simple riff by using a hammer-on to a chord tone from an open string, as in the second beat of **Example 6**. Hammer on to the second fret of the fifth string, then move to the open

Adding short riffs between chords can often make things more interesting, particularly between verses of a song, or when there is no other melody to draw listeners' attention.

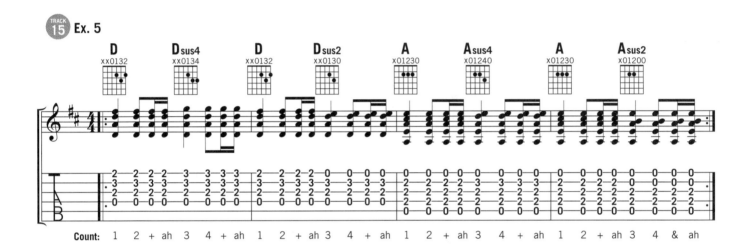

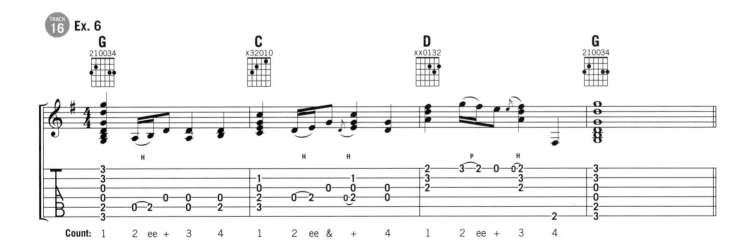

fourth string—two notes that are part of the C chord you played on beat one.

You can also construct riffs with notes that are not in the chords. **Example 7** shows some simple riffs over C, F, and G chords. The A notes in measures 2 and 6 are not part of the C and G chords, and the D note in measure 4 is not part of the F chord, but they all sound good, don't they? Over C, the A is called a sixth, and over G, it's a ninth. The D over F is another sixth. As you play, pay attention to the way these melody notes interact with the underlying chords.

Practice these examples slowly, making sure each note rings out clearly. If you've never played hammer-ons and pull-offs within chords before, it can take a new kind of coordina-tion—you might notice that you need to arch your fingers differently so you don't mute any of the strings.

The 16-measure accompaniment to "**Bury Me Beneath the Willow**" includes many of the ideas shown in these examples. Notice the bass runs in measures 6 and 13, which lead from G to D, and the bass run in measure 14, which leads back to G. Measure 7 features a Dsus4 chord that helps relieve the monotony of two full bars of D, followed by a quick F♯ note that leads back to the G chord. Remember to take things slowly at first and play each measure in time—even with these added fills and runs, good rhythm playing still requires the ability to keep a steady beat.

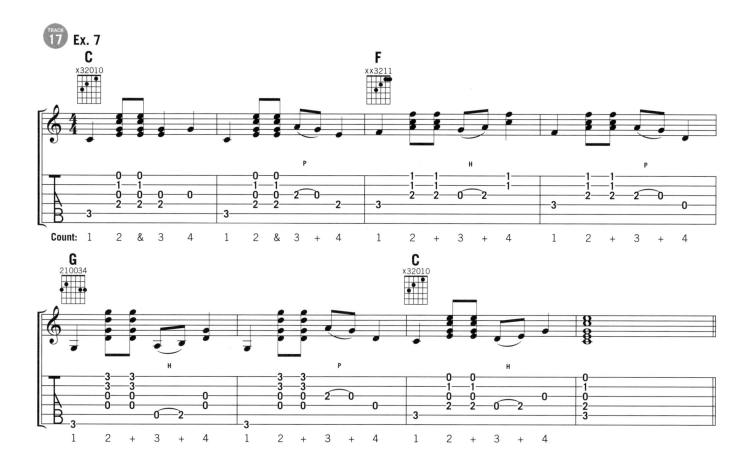

RHYTHM GUITAR ESSENTIALS

Bury Me Beneath the Willow

Traditional, arranged by Karen Hogg

ROCK RHYTHM FILLS

Andrew DuBrock

If you want to play rhythm guitar in a band or accompany your voice, you've probably been learning how to hold down a steady rhythm or simple strum pattern. But playing the same patterns throughout an entire song can start to sound and feel pretty boring. How can you spice things up a little? One way is to add some rhythm fills to your backup.

A fill is anything that fills a space between a phrase or section of a song. The series of tom hits the drummer plays going into a chorus is a fill, the lick a lead guitarist plays between vocal phrases is a fill, and the flurry of high notes the bass player hits on the way back to the verse is also a fill. Not surprisingly, you can play fills on rhythm guitar as well.

Let's take a look at a basic rhythm fill. **Example 1** shows a simple strum pattern on a D chord. If you've been strumming this pattern throughout a song, all you have to do to turn it into a rhythm fill is to vary the rhythm so that it stands out in relation to the measures surrounding it. **Example 2** shows the easiest way to vary the rhythm: by simply leaving out an eighth note. In this case, I've left out the eighth note on beat three. If we put this measure in the context of a progression (**Example 3**) using the strum pattern from Example 1, you can see how that missing eighth note makes the measure stand out. The key here is to note that context is everything. To prove that point, we could even take the basic strum pattern from Example 1 and make that a rhythm fill. Check out **Example 4** to see how this works. In com-

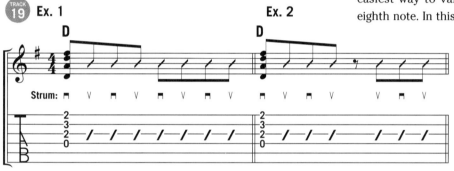

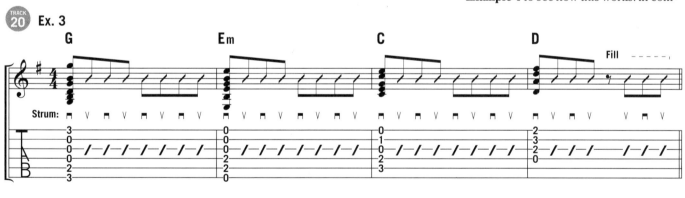

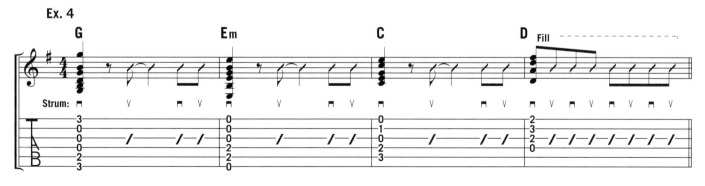

parison to the first three measures of Example 4, that basic strum pattern does sound like a fill.

Put a Fill in a Song

Now that you know what a rhythm fill is, let's take a look at a few ways of applying this concept and see how guitarists have used rhythm fills in songs. **Example 5** shows how something simple with heavy accents can work well as a rhythm fill. This is similar to what John Lennon played coming back into the verse of "Norwegian Wood." Again, notice how the context makes the fill stand out. The fill is a contrast to the strumming pattern in the measures leading up to the accents on the A chord. Don't let the 16th notes or the 6/8 time signature scare

you. Count "one two three four five six" along with the notes in the notation if you have problems.

In **Example 6**, I've taken a strum pattern similar to something Ryan Adams might play and fashioned a rhythmic fill in the final measure. Again, don't let the 16th notes scare you. The trickiest part of this rhythm pattern is the accents, which fall alternately on down- and upstrokes. It may help to count it aloud ("one-ee-and-a two-ee-and-a three-ee-and-a four-ee-and-a"). Notice that the fill has the same rhythm as the accented notes of the previous measures, but by leaving out the 16th notes between those accented notes, you've subtly altered the pattern and created a fill.

Another way to create a fill is to strum some harmonics. Ani DiFranco often uses this technique, and **Example 7** shows

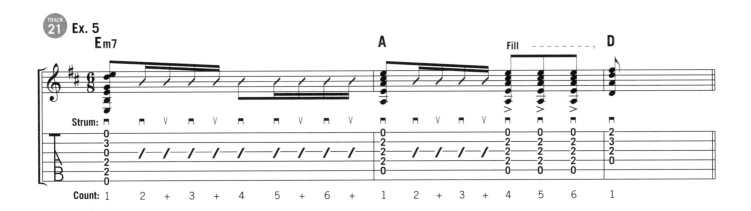

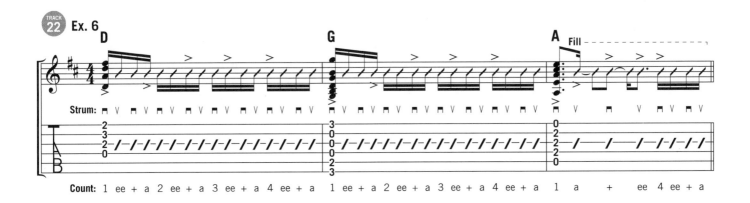

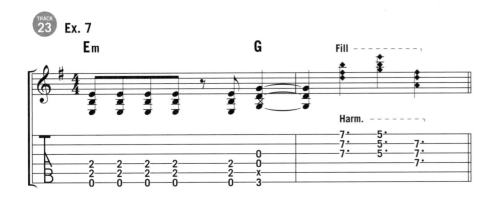

a fill similar to something she might play. Easily accessible harmonics are found at the fifth, seventh, and 12th frets. If you're not familiar with harmonics, lightly touch the string directly over the fret (not behind it, as you would with a fretted note), pluck the string with your right hand, and immediately lift your left hand off the strings to let the harmonic ring out. Try playing around with these in the context of whatever tune you're playing.

Add a Chord

Sometimes adding another chord or two to a rhythm fill can help. **Example 8** shows the end of a phrase in G. Notice how **Example 9** takes this phrase and quickly touches on C in measure 3 to make a nice fill. This is similar to what the Indigo Girls do before the chorus of "Closer to Fine."

Joni Mitchell also uses this idea in "Big Yellow Taxi." **Examples 10** and **11** show a pattern similar to what Mitchell plays but in standard tuning (a tuning she rarely uses).

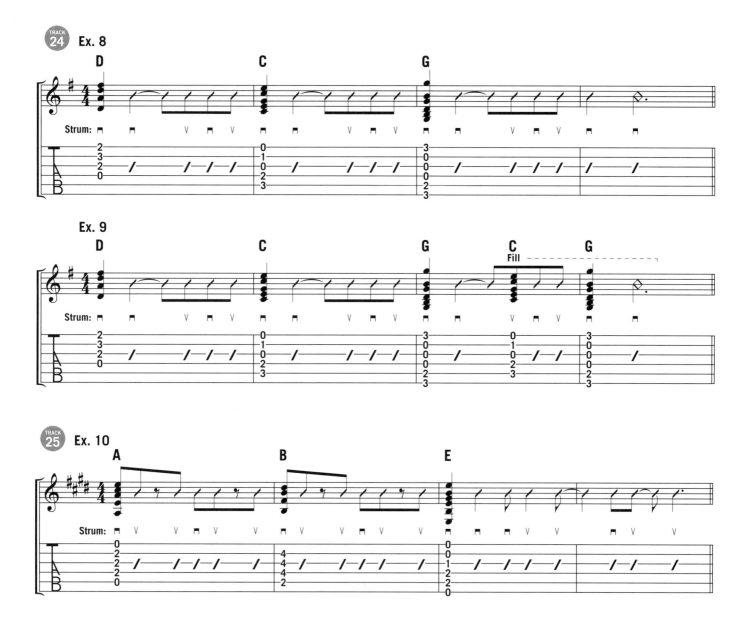

RHYTHM GUITAR ESSENTIALS

Example 10 shows the basic progression, and Example 11 adds a rhythm fill à la Joni. Note that you're changing to two different chords here.

And if you want to get really crazy, check out some of Pete Townshend's rhythm work. **Example 12** shows a progression similar to a phrase in the Who's "Behind Blue Eyes." Now look at **Example 13** to see the way Townshend might turn the final measure into an amazing fill. He creates a lot of the driving accents here by using downstrokes.

Before you get carried away, remember that you're playing songs—sometimes with other people! If you deviate from the chord progression too much (or even slightly), you're going to conflict with the bass player and the other instruments. So this technique should be used sparingly and with a little planning. Be sure to try out any new chord fills with the rest of your band to see if they work.

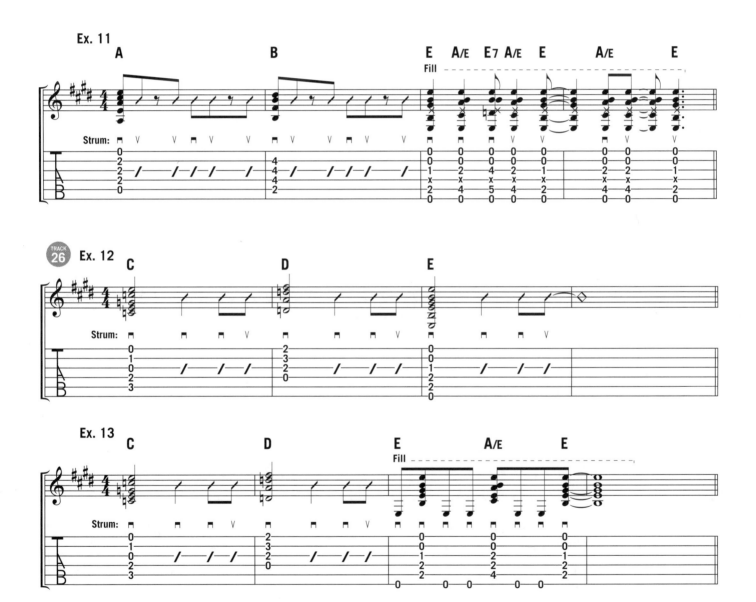

Practice Your Fills

Now that you have a few tools for creating your own rhythm fills, a good way to practice them is by taking a progression and playing it over and over while experimenting with fills. It could be a song you're working on or just a progression your fingers find. **Example 14** shows an extended example of how you might do this over a D–D/F♯–G–A7sus4 progression. This example uses all the techniques we've covered in this lesson. See if you can pick out each one, and then try coming up with some of your own.

Remember that rhythm guitar isn't rocket science, and your goal shouldn't be to make everyone notice your rhythm playing. The best rhythm players serve the music at hand and are noticed most when they're missing. Your first job as a rhythm guitarist is to hold down the groove. These fills are ways you can spice up your playing between vocal phrases, at transitions, and between sections. But always remember that you're not playing a rhythm solo! Your fills will be most memorable when the listener only notices them on occasion.

LEFT-HAND MUTING

David Hamburger

Strumming's great, and once you can move smoothly from chord to chord there are a million songs you can play with that wide-open, down-and-up kind of strumming. But chances are you've run across songs that don't sound quite right when you just strum the open chords. If you want to put a little more of a percussive groove into your playing, you may want to check out the sound of left-hand muting. The name explains what it's all about: muting the strings with your left hand. But the question is, how? And the next question is, when?

Let's start with **Example 1**—a basic down-and-up strum on an open D-major chord. Let your left-hand thumb drift up over the top of the neck to mute the low E string so you can just wail away on the remaining five strings.

While your other fingers are in a D chord position, mute the strings by resting your pinky on the strings without pressing down.

Your pinky should still be free if you're fingering the D chord with your index, middle, and ring fingers. Lay your pinky down across all six strings (if you can—if not, the top five strings will do as long as you're still muting the low string with your left-hand thumb). Just rest your pinky on the strings (see photo), without pressing down at all. Don't fret anything with your pinky; just mute the strings.

Now strum the D chord like you did before. **Example 2** shows what this looks like in tab and notation. You should just hear the sound of the pick scratching all six strings with no chord sounding.

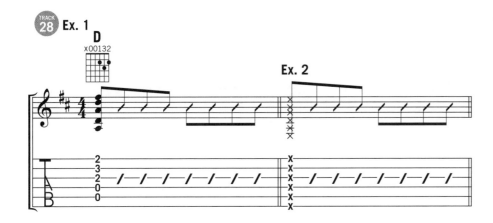

Now let's alternate between the pinky muting and the open strum. Begin by alternating each measure (**Example 3**). Next, switch between open and muted strings every two beats, as in **Example 4**. Then try switching every two strokes (**Example 5**).

Try Other Chords

You can use this technique with any other open chord that can be fretted with just three fingers. Try it on an A chord (**Example 6**) and an E chord (**Example 7**). It will also work on any of the following open chords: Am, Am7, A7, C, D7, Dm7, E7, Em7, and the "small" F.

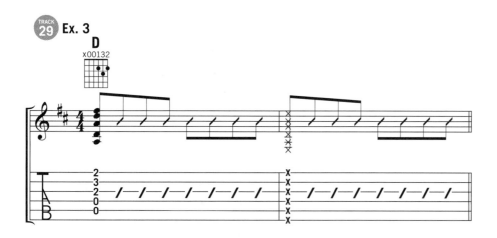

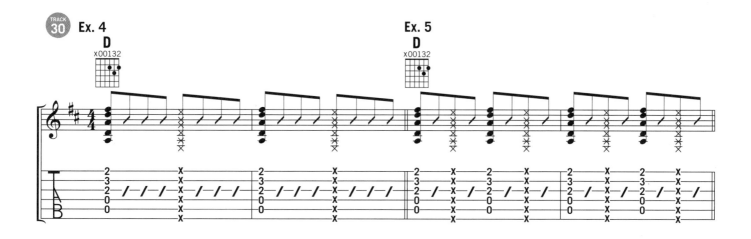

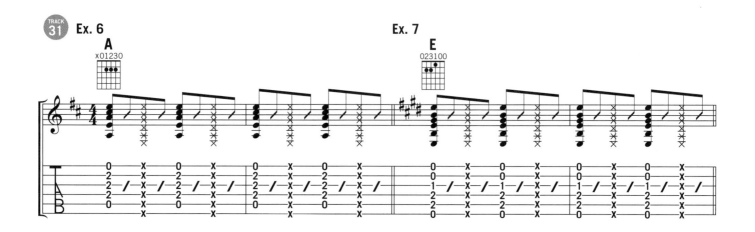

Of course, to apply this technique to a song you'll need to be able to put these moves into action while changing from chord to chord. Start by alternating between the A and D chords while continuing to mute the strings with your left hand on every other beat (**Example 8**). Try any other combinations you can think of using the open chords listed above: Am to E7, Dm to F, C to A7, etc.

Another Way to Mute

You may have noticed that there are a few common open chords—G, B7, and C7, in particular—missing from this list.

These chords don't lend themselves to this technique, because you can't mute the strings with your pinky if you're using it to play one of the notes in the chord. But there is another way to get the same effect on these three renegade voicings. Have you ever tried to get a dog on a leash to go somewhere he doesn't want to go? You know what happens: the dog digs in his paws, leans backward, and eventually collapses to the floor, becoming impossible to move. Your fingers are going to do a similar collapse to the fretboard. Form a first-position G chord with your ring finger on the low string.

To mute the chord with your left hand, begin by relaxing your grip on the fretboard so you're just touching the strings with your fingertips, not pressing down. Next, let your ring finger collapse so that it lies flat across all six strings—touching them without pressing them to the fretboard. Your other fingers will flatten out somewhat as well; keep them in place so that when you grab the chord again you can make it ring out clearly.

Try playing a couple of measures of G, alternating between open and muted strums (**Example 9**). For C7 and B7, begin by relaxing your grip; this takes care of muting four of the six strings. Next, tilt your hand slightly toward the high strings. In the case of C7, your index finger will come to rest on the first string, keeping it from ringing out. For B7, this tilt of the hand will bring your ring finger into contact with the second string, muting it. For both chords, you'll need to keep your thumb above the edge of the fretboard, so you can use it to mute the sixth string. Try muting these chords in **Examples 10** and **11**.

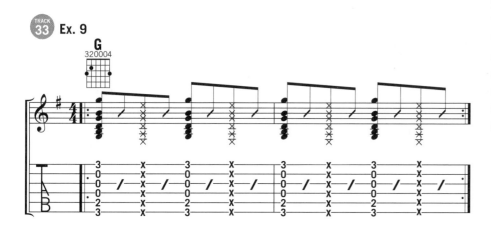

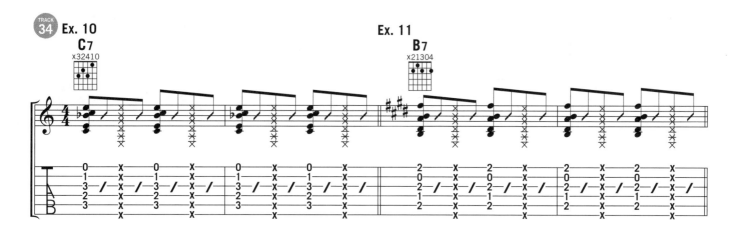

Vary the Muting

So far we've just used one strumming pattern: alternating beats of unmuted and muted chords. The next step is to see how you can vary the muting in a single bar. For starters, let's unmute two more strums in the measure. In **Example 12**, you're just muting the A chord on the second and fourth downstrokes (beats two and four) in the measure. Try this pattern on something like the Beatles' "Ob-La-Di, Ob-La-Da" and check out the kick it gives to a basic down-and-up strum pattern.

For a great shuffle rhythm, take the pattern in Example 12 and play it with a swing feel. Try it on an E chord (**Example 13**), then apply it to a Chicago blues like "Bright Lights, Big City" or a country shuffle like Ray Price's "Invitation to the Blues."

Leaving out downstrokes or upstrokes is another way to expand your collection of strums. **Example 14** omits the first upstroke in Example 12; take it out for a spin on something like Neil Young's "Heart of Gold." Tweaking the second half of the measure yields another worthwhile pattern, one where most

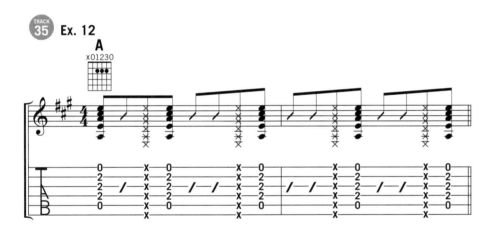

TRACK 35 **Ex. 12**

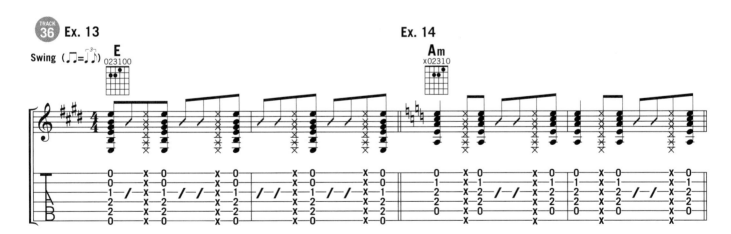

TRACK 36 **Ex. 13**

Ex. 14

of what you hear is upstrokes. Try out **Example 15** at a fairly uptempo clip, and see how it sounds on a song like Paul Simon's "Kodachrome."

Of course, the king of all scratchy guitar rhythms is the Bo Diddley beat, named for the rock 'n' roll pioneer whose all-time coolness is certified by the fact that he toured with a maraca player. **Example 16** stretches things out to a two-bar rhythmic pattern—think of the Rolling Stones' version of "Not Fade Away" for further sonic clues on how this groove should sound.

Put It Together

Finally, let's close with a complete song. The traditional blues tune "**I Know You Rider**" was a 1960s folk revival favorite, with John Renbourn, Hot Tuna, and the Grateful Dead all recording interpretations. Our version uses a two-bar strumming pattern that has muted downstrokes on the second and fourth downbeats in the first measure and muted downbeats on the first and second downbeats of the second measure. But the longer strums on beats three and four of the second measure really give this tune its characteristic sound.

Start by just hanging on a chord or two while you get the muting of the two-bar strum pattern in order. Once you've got the feel of the groove in your hands, try tackling two or four measures of the song at a time. As with all of these patterns, the sooner you can get your hands to function on autopilot, the sooner you can direct your attention to the chord progression and the song as a whole.

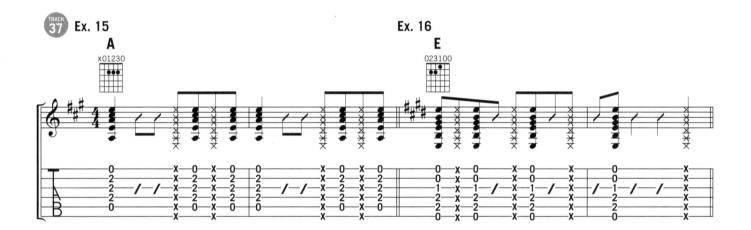

I Know You Rider

Traditional, arranged by David Hamburger

RHYTHM GUITAR ESSENTIALS

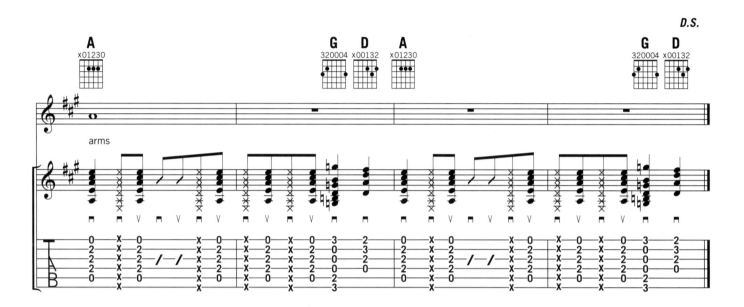

```
        A                 G      D       A  G D A
1.  I know you rider gonna miss me when I'm gone

                        G        D       A  G D A
    I know you rider gonna miss me when I'm gone

        G      D       G      D     A  G D A G D
    Gonna miss your baby from rolling in your arms


        A                 G      D       A  G D A
2.  Lay down last night but I could not take my rest

                        G        D       A  G D A
    Lay down last night but I could not take my rest

    G      D         G         D    A  G D A G D
    My mind was wandering like the wild geese in the west


        A                 G      D       A  G D A
3.  The sun's gonna shine on my backdoor some day

                        G        D       A  G D A
    The sun's gonna shine on my backdoor some day

    G          D        G        D      A  G D A G D
    The wind's gonna rise, blow all my troubles away


        A                 G      D     A  G D A
4.  I wish I was a headlight on a northbound train

                        G      D     A  G D A
    I wish I was a headlight on a northbound train

    G        D          G        D    A G D A G D
    I'd shine my light through the cool Colorado rain
```

SIMPLE SYNCOPATED GROOVES

Andrew DuBrock

Guitarists often focus so much on left-hand fingerings that they forget how important the right hand is. You can play the fanciest stuff in the world with your left hand, but if it doesn't groove, it's not going to sound as good as the simplest rhythm track played well. And one of the most important parts of laying down a solid groove is getting comfortable playing with syncopation, the funky sound you get when you squeeze notes in between the beats.

Let's start by playing some plain vanilla rhythms that don't involve syncopation. Play through **Example 1**, making sure to use downstrokes on all of the beats. If it sounds boring, then you're doing just fine! Now try strumming through the eighth-note rhythm in **Example 2**. This time, alternate between downstrokes and upstrokes. Count the beats aloud as you play them, and repeat this measure a few times until your right hand gets into a groove. There are four beats in these measures (counted one, two, three, four), and the notes between each beat are counted as *and*, so the full measure goes like this: one-and two-and three-and four-and.

To start syncopating that rhythm, go to **Example 3** and play through the measure as you did in Example 2, this time

leaving out the downstroke on beat two. The important thing here is not to let the syncopations alter the groove. Your right hand should keep a steady tempo and feel, even though you're not playing a steady stream of eighth notes. How do you do that? If you stop to think about which way your pick is moving, you've probably already lost the groove. Or, if you pause after that first upstroke—waiting for the right moment to strum up again—you're going to have a hard time keeping the groove steady. The easiest way to get it going is to keep your right hand moving constantly up and down. Start by strumming in the air above the strings and then connect with the guitar strings on the down- or upstrokes you want to hear, while keeping the rhythm going in the air in between.

So in Example 3, you play a silent downstroke on beat two and strum the strings on all the other notes in the measure. Keep repeating this measure until you get the hang of it. Some people call this pendulum strumming, because your arm is moving constantly up and down like a pendulum.

Example 4 goes a step further, subtracting the downstrokes on beats two, three, and four. The trickiest part of this measure is when you go back to the beginning. Notice that the final upstroke

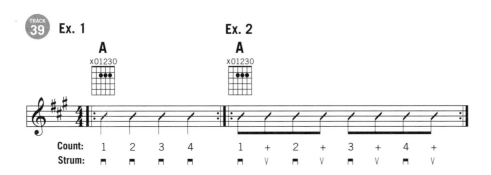

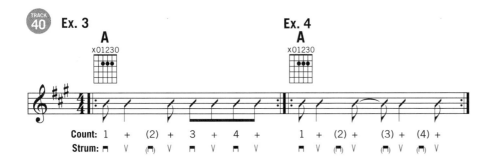

in the measure is immediately followed by the only downstroke. Play through this one for a while until you're comfortable with it. Again, try counting along, remembering that you'll be strumming when you say "one" and every time you say *and*.

Syncopate a Progression

Let's put some of this funky syncopation to use. **Example 5** shows a chord progression you might use as a riff or backup for a tune. Notice that it sounds stiff because there's absolutely no syncopation. **Example 6** takes this progression and dresses it up a little by anticipating most of the chord changes, playing

them with an upstroke before the downbeat. A simple change like this can make a progression sound much more hip.

This type of syncopation can be heard all over the place. **Example 7** shows a syncopated progression reminiscent of the old Creedence Clearwater Revival song "Proud Mary." The change between the A and C chords in the last measure is kind of tricky. To make it a little easier, try playing only the bass note of the first A chord. **Example 8** is a riff reminiscent of the Beatles' classic "You Won't See Me." In this example, most of the notes should be very short. Try damping the strings with your right hand between chords or lifting your left-hand fingers off the strings a little and using a finger that isn't fretting any strings to mute the rest.

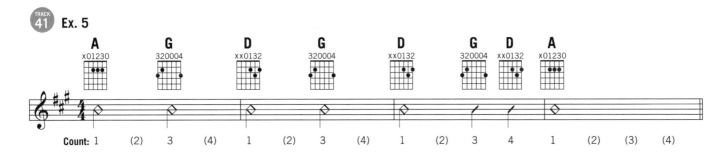

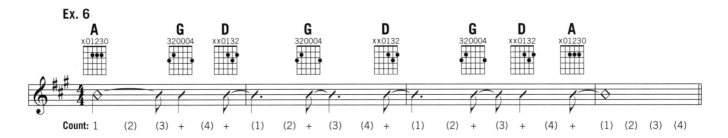

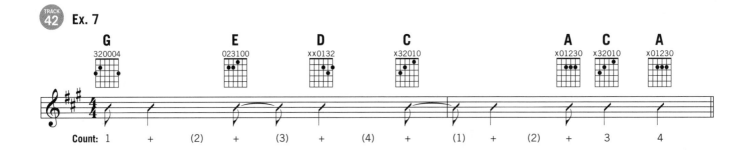

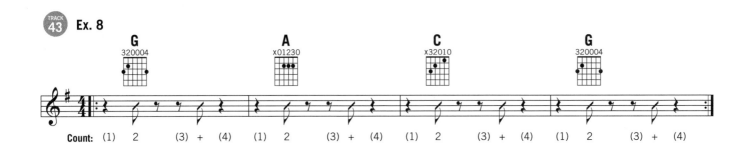

Syncopate and Repeat

Another way of thinking about syncopation is to take a simple rhythmic idea that doesn't quite fit into the regular pulse and repeat that idea to create a line. Since the idea is a little out of whack to begin with, repeating it makes it fall against the beat in interesting ways. For instance, if you take a phrase like the one in **Example 9** and repeat it four times, it takes three full measures to complete a cycle (**Example 10**) and you get some pretty interesting rhythms. Make sure to count the beats and really hear where the one is. **Example 11** uses this rhythm in a single-note melody. Sometimes it sounds even better if you don't cycle all the way through the pattern; I like the way **Example 12** cuts the same line short by a measure.

> *Another way of thinking about syncopation is to take a simple rhythmic idea that doesn't quite fit into the regular pulse and repeat that idea to create a line.*

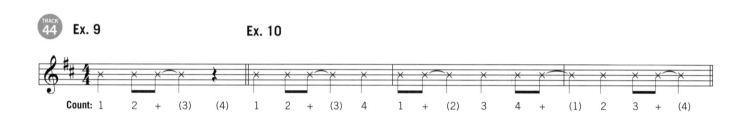

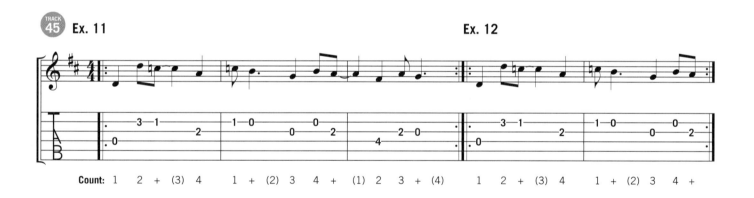

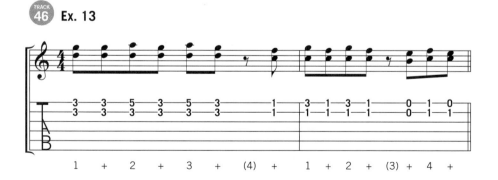

Syncopation in riffs and single-note lines is found in all kinds of music. **Example 13** shows how syncopation is used in a riff similar to the one in the Sugar Ray tune "Every Morning." **Example 14** is a riff emulating another Beatles classic, "I Feel Fine," that uses this same kind of syncopation.

Add an Accent

Keep in mind that syncopation isn't always about subtracting beats; you can also strum through all of the beats, putting the accent on odd beats, as shown in **Example 15**. Be sure to really bring out the accented notes and strum very lightly on the unaccented ones.

For a look at how this type of syncopation can be used, see **Example 16**, an example of how Celtic guitar ace John Doyle might back up a tune with syncopated strumming. In this situation, the unaccented strums are not very important, and it really doesn't matter if you hit the strings for each of these strokes; it is important, however, that you connect strongly on all of the accented strums.

"'N Sink" incorporates some of the ideas from these examples into a short piece that should help you fine-tune your syncopation chops. The first two measures use a single-note line that takes advantage of offbeat syncopation similar to the rhythms in Example 4. The fifth, sixth, ninth, and tenth measures use the same kind of syncopated strumming found in Examples 15 and 16; make sure to accent the underlined beats. The final three measures thicken the opening phrase with some full chords, making it sound more like the Beatles-ish riff in Example 14.

If you have trouble with any of the phrases, isolate them, slow them down, and count the beats aloud until you get the groove. You can also add some syncopation into chord progressions, riffs, and tunes you already know. It doesn't have to be complicated to sound great; sometimes just one well-placed accent can help a stuffed shirt hang loose.

TRACK 47 **Ex. 14**

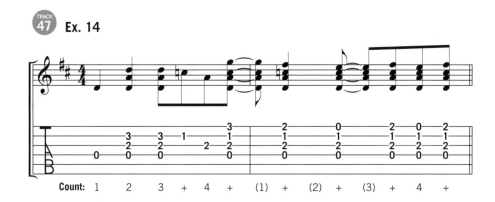

TRACK 48 **Ex. 15**

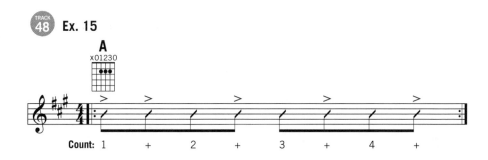

TRACK 49 **Ex. 16**

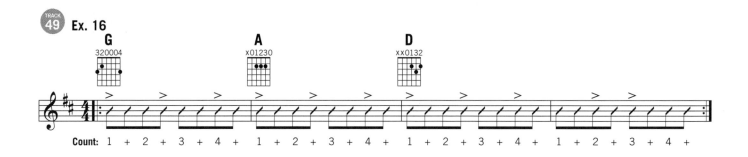

'N Sink

Music by Andrew DuBrock

PLAY IN A DIFFERENT TIME

David Hodge

Have you ever tried to play a song but been completely stumped by the rhythm? It might not be you—it could be that the song is in a timing that you've never played in before.

Most songs that you hear and play are in 4/4 time. They have the familiar, steady, pulsing count of "one two three four," so that's what you strum. But some songs are in a different time signature. Their pulse is measured in twos or threes, so your strumming has to take this into account. In this lesson, we'll look at rhythms based on a pulse of three (or groups of three) and see how easily and quickly we can adapt to these new time signatures.

If you've got a handle on basic strumming and first-position chords, it shouldn't take you too long to master these rhythms. Your biggest obstacle will be getting your brain to stop thinking in 4/4 time. If your metronome has settings for different time signatures, use it to help you internalize the counts. Count out loud along with your playing until you feel comfortable with the exercises.

Waltz Along

Listen to Paul Simon's "America" or Billy Joel's "Piano Man," and you'll immediately hear the pulse of 3/4 timing. Waltzes are slow 3/4 songs, and dancers use smooth, graceful movements to get from the first beat of one measure to the first beat of the next. (Think of the scenes in classic Disney cartoons when the princess and prince finally dance together—it's usually a waltz.) When you count in 3/4, give the first beat the accent: "*one* two three, *one* two three."

Now let's translate this rhythm to the guitar. Start with three downstrokes on the A chord, as shown in **Example 1**. Don't be shy about counting aloud so you can keep the three-beat pulse at the front of your brain. When you're comfortable with the general rhythm, replace the second beat with two eighth notes (strum down then up) as in **Example 2**. Or use eighth notes for both the second and third beats (**Example 3**). Easy, right?

You can also use your boom-chuck rhythms in 3/4, but I suppose it becomes more of a boom-chuck-chuck. Just strum twice after each bass note, as in **Example 4**, which uses an A chord. **Example 5** gives you an

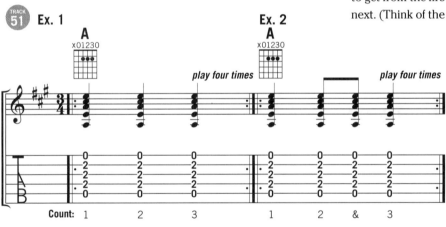

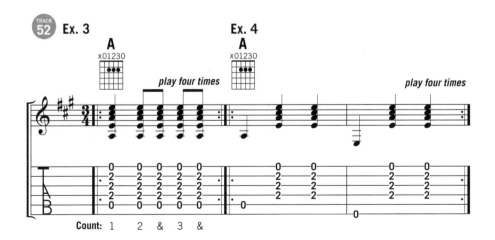

alternating bass line using both A and D chords. You can use either of these patterns to play a song like "I'm So Lonesome I Could Cry."

Play a Rhythmic Six-Pack

This same three-beat pulse also turns up in 6/8 time, which you can hear in rock and pop songs like "Norwegian Wood" by the Beatles and "Breaking the Girl" by the Red Hot Chili Peppers. In 6/8, each measure has six beats and the eighth note is counted as one beat. You can count 6/8 two different ways, either as two triplets ("one-and-a two-and-a") or in groups of six ("one two three four five six"). Both ways are fine. Try out 6/8 time in **Example 6**.

Don't be intimidated by all the 16th notes you'll run into in 6/8. Remember that eighth notes are one beat, so 16th notes are half beats. Try **Example 7**, counting "one two-and three four five-and six." For **Example 8**, count like this: "one two-and three-and four five-and six-and."

SONGS IN A DIFFERENT TIME

These songs are great examples of what can happen when you go beyond 4/4 and into more nonstandard time signatures.

3/4 Stephen Stills, "Change Partners" Elliott Smith, "Waltz #2"

6/8 Pearl Jam, "Nothing Man," "Elderly Woman Behind the Counter in a Small Town"

9/8 Leo Kottke, Bach's "Jesu, Joy of Man's Desiring"

12/8 Stevie Ray Vaughan, "The Sky Is Crying"

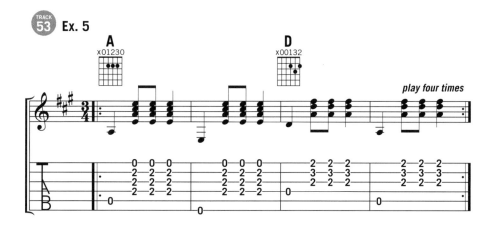

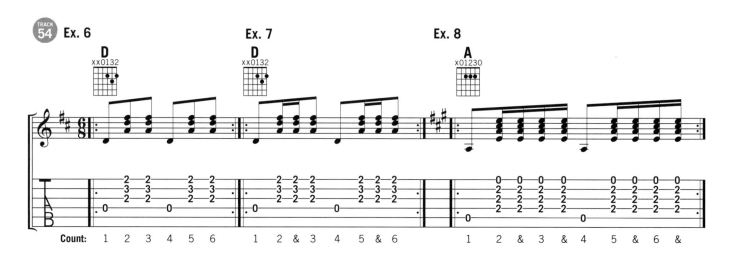

When you're up to a little more of a challenge, give **Example 9** a try. The Red Hot Chili Peppers' John Frusciante makes these kinds of syncopated rhythms sound easy; that's part of what makes him such a great guitarist. You already know how to play the second half of this measure, so concentrate on the first three beats. Strum on the first beat, then the upstroke of the second beat, then the upstroke of the third beat ("one _-and _-and four five-and six"). Again, count out loud as you're playing these examples; it will really help you get these rhythms.

Take Five, Seven, or 12

While the Beatles' "You've Got to Hide Your Love Away" is technically in 4/4 time, each beat is played as a triplet, giving it a similar three-beat pulse to the other rhythms we've played. Slow blues songs are often written in 12/8 timing in order to convey this triplet feel (as in 6/8, the eighth notes are counted as one beat, but there are 12 beats per measure).

Should you ever find yourself playing in truly complex time signatures, like 5/4 (think Dave Brubeck's "Take Five") or 7/4 ("Money" by Pink Floyd), it will be easier if you break the measures down into manageable parts of twos, threes, and fours. **Example 10** shows you a 5/4 rhythm, which is played as if it's one measure of 3/4 followed by one measure of 2/4.

So the next time you hear a song with a triplet pulse, don't hesitate to pick up your guitar and play along. Getting the right rhythm pattern is truly as simple as "one, two, three."

READING TIME SIGNATURES

Sheet music will always tell you what time signature a song is in by giving you the time signature: the fraction right at the beginning of a piece of music.

4 How many beats are in each measure

4 Which note counts as one beat (2=half note, 4=quarter note, 8=eighth note, etc.)

Here's how to count the beats in common time signatures. Half beats are always counted as *ands* between the numbers:

If you use a metronome (and you should!), remember that the click of the metronome can be what you want it to be. We usually think of each click as a beat, but you can use it to mark the first beat of each group of two, three, or four beats. For example, in 6/8, you might find it easier to count "click two three click five six." Some metronomes also have settings for these different time signatures.

TRACK 55 **Ex. 9**

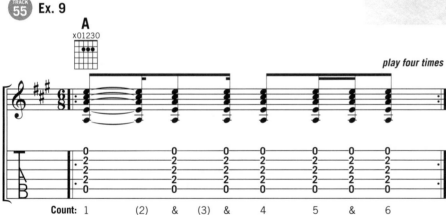

TRACK 56 **Ex. 10**

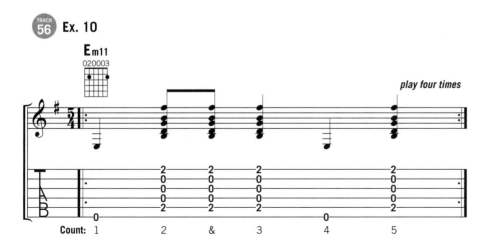

SIX WAYS TO EXPAND YOUR RHYTHM

Andrew DuBrock

Every player reaches plateaus, where you pick up the guitar, go to the same place on the neck, and play the same types of chord shapes and rhythms. In this lesson, we'll look at six concrete ways for getting out of rhythmic ruts. We'll even take a few hints from pop-rock rhythm masters like Dave Matthews, John Mayer, and Willy Porter.

1. SUBSTITUTE EXTENDED CHORDS FOR SIMPLE SHAPES.

A quick way to instill life into a less-than-inspiring chord progression is by using extended chords. Say you have a simple Bm–E–A–D progression like the one in **Example 1**. This progression sounds pretty cool but still feels a bit "vanilla" for the backdrop of a song. If you substitute extended chord shapes (sevenths, ninths, and up, along with suspended chords), it really fills out the sound. John Mayer brought a progression like this to a new place in his hit "Daughters" by using shapes up the neck mixed with open strings to create lush extended chords similar to what you see in **Example 2**. Up at the sev-

enth fret, the blander Bm–Em–A–D chord progression becomes Bm11–E7–A9–D6(9).

2. ADD BASS LINES.

Bass lines aren't only meant for bass guitars. Try adding bass lines to one-chord vamps or complete progressions; if you're playing with a bass player, he or she can always stick to the roots and backbeat. Dave Matthews used this concept to perfection in his mid-'90s hit "Crash Into Me" with a bass line similar to that in **Example 3**.

Notice how the fingers are parked in an E5 shape on the top four strings throughout the progression, even though the bass line underneath implies a changing chord progression.

3. DEVELOP SHORT THEMES INTO COMPLETE IDEAS.

One of my favorite techniques is to come up with a theme and try to incorporate that into a chord progression or riff.

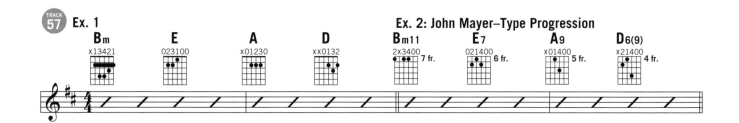

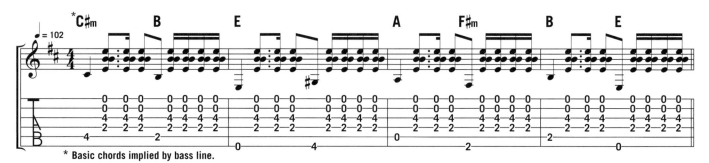

* Basic chords implied by bass line.

Example 4 shows a basic melodic idea I wanted to incorporate into an F#m–D–A–E–G–D–A chord progression. If you look at this melodic idea and think about how it fits with each of the above chords, you'll see that its last note (A) is a chord tone in every chord of the progression except for the E and G chords. This means it'll probably sound good ending on each of the other chords, but we may need to modify it a little bit for those E and G chords. By changing the last note in the phrase to a B note over both the E and G chords, I had the riff to my song "Mark" (**Example 5**).

4. PLAY SINGLE-NOTE RHYTHM.

You don't have to strum chords all the time to play effective rhythm guitar. Single-note riffs can be a fine rhythmic foundation, and you can develop simple lines into complete ideas with a little bit of work. Take **Example 6**, for instance—the main theme to my song "Into This Night." I came up with the riff in the first measure, really liked it, and wanted to develop

it further. I thought the riff would sound good repeated once, followed by a Bm–C–D progression, then repeated again at the end. It was tough to come up with a similar single-note pattern that worked over that part of the progression—tough enough that, once I came up with this example, I had to pull out a

KEEP IT STEADY

Having great rhythm doesn't only mean you can play complicated rhythmic patterns. It's surprising how many excellent guitarists have a poor sense of rhythm. The best rhythm players have an inner sense of rhythm that stays constant no matter how difficult (or easy) the rhythm they're playing is. Sometimes the simplest rhythms are the toughest to play in time *without* sounding like a robot. Play with a metronome, play with other musicians, and even play along with recordings to continue developing a steady inner sense of rhythm.

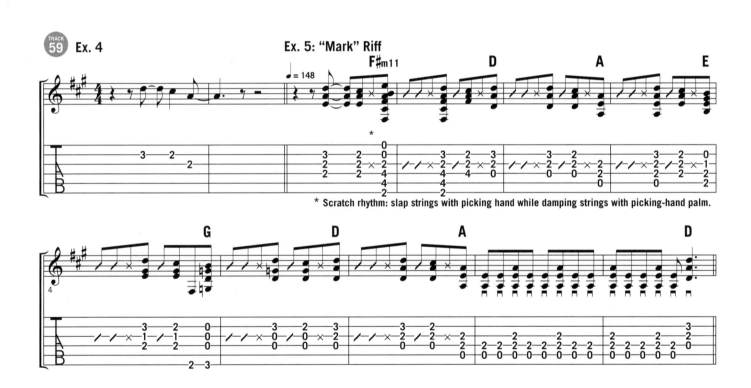

Ex. 4   Ex. 5: "Mark" Riff

* Scratch rhythm: slap strings with picking hand while damping strings with picking-hand palm.

Ex. 6: Single-Note Rhythm from "Into This Night"

metronome and break it down to a near stop to even begin playing it! You know you're really stretching when you come up with something that you have to practice at a crawl before you can play it up to speed.

5. TRY AN ALTERNATE TUNING.

Alternate tunings can kick start your creativity and give you a whole new palette of sounds. Peter Mulvey and Willy Porter are known for their alternate tunings, multiple capos, and low, low bass lines. Try tuning your low E string way down to B or even lower, and use that string exclusively for playing bass lines. You can go into a distant alternate tuning, as well, but sometimes just one simple string tweak does the trick. I popped my A string down to B and was immediately inspired to come up with the verse/chorus progression for my song "I Keep Coming Back for You" (**Example 7**).

6. CHANGE CHORDS AT DIFFERENT TIMES.

In John Mayer's "Daughters," the verse and chorus progressions are nearly identical, but the chord changes shift from one chord per measure during the verses to two chords per measure over the chorus. By speeding up his chord changes,

Mayer was able to create a completely new song with one chord progression. In my song "**Into This Night**," I vary the lengths of chord changes. Notice how many measures have one chord with a quick one-beat chord on the last beat of the measure. On the chorus, I pick up the pace by changing chords more frequently—especially in measure 20, where I play a new chord on each beat. Try other chord-change variations as well. Switch chords on the offbeat, play some chords for partial measures, or try allowing different chords to have different rhythmic lengths.

Listen

Music is all about communicating sound, so make sure you listen to what you're playing. You don't have to be a theory guru to come up with complicated or interesting chords. John Mayer's progression in "Daughters" most likely was inspired by one cool shape and letting the fingers walk down slowly. Try something new, listen to what you're playing, and hear where you want it to go. If you have two chords and you hear one note in the middle of those chords that wants to go somewhere else, try it. See where it leads you, and you will be well on your way.

TRACK 61   **E A D G A E Tuning**

TRACK 62   **Ex. 7: Alternate Tuning for "I Keep Coming Back for You"**
Tuning: E A D G A E

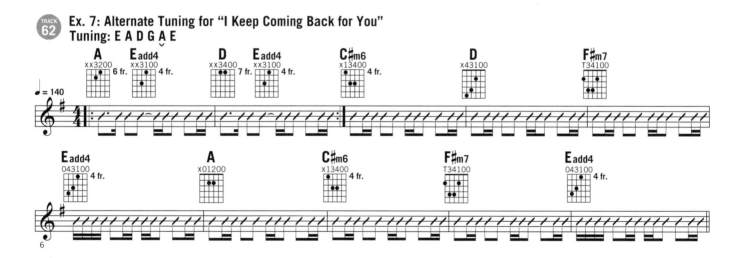

Into This Night

Words and music by Andrew DuBrock

1. There's a

Verse

hun - dred ques - tions in your eyes your eyes in your

2–3. *See additional lyrics.*

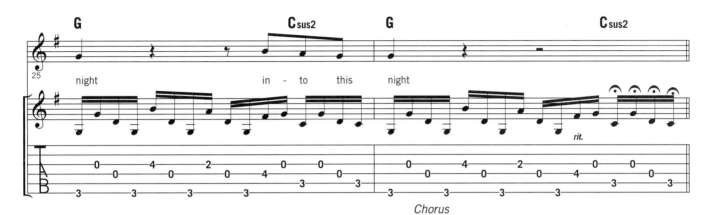

Csus2   G   Csus2 G Csus2 Bm C D G
1. There's a hundred questions in your eyes, your eyes, in your eyes

Csus2   G   Csus2 G Csus2 Bm   C D G
There's a hundred answers in my hands, my hands, in my hands

      Chorus
      D   Csus2 F6(9) G
And I hope that we can see this through

      D   G/B Csus2 G D   G   Csus2 G
For I will not carry you into this night

   Csus2 G   Csus2 G Csus2 Bm C D   G
2. We sit here frozen by the shining moon, bright moon, bright moon

Csus2   G   Csus2 G Csus2 Bm C D   G
Hours of silence filling up the room, the room, the empty room

Chorus
      D   Csus2 F6(9) G
And I hope tomorrow brings the truth

      D   G/B Csus2 G D   G   Csus2 G
For I will not carry you into this night

Csus2   G   Csus2 G Csus2 Bm C D G
3. There's a hint of sadness in your sigh, your sigh, in your sigh

Csus2   G   Csus2 G Csus2 Bm C D G
There's no sound to give away my mind, my mind, my mind

      Chorus
      D   Csus2 F6(9) G
It gets so dark I can't see where to move

         D G/B Csus2 G Dadd4   G   Csus2
I pray that I don't carry you into this night

LESS IS MORE

Jeffrey Pepper Rodgers

As we progress on guitar, we naturally want to learn how to make basic chords sound bigger, by adding jazzy extensions, for instance, or using alternate tunings to expand the instrument's range. But in many musical situations, it's more effective to take the opposite approach: creating fresh chord sounds by playing fewer notes and fewer strings. In this lesson we'll look at ways to reduce standard chord fingerings and then try them in a simple progression and a full song.

Play Fewer Notes

Start by strumming through the familiar open-position chords in **Example 1**. These forms have all the ingredients of the chord—roots, thirds, and fifths—arranged in a voicing you've heard a gazillion times. Let's try taking out a note: the third, which is what makes the chord major (if it's a major third interval from the root) or minor (a minor third from the root). Why remove this important and perfectly good note? Because

its absence makes the chord more open-ended—it could lean toward minor or major or a more complex harmonic flavor depending on what is going on in the melody and other instruments.

Example 2 shows a few ways to play G, D, C, A, and E chords without thirds. These are known as 5 chords, since they contain just roots and fifths. In some fingerings, you need to mute a string by leaning a finger against it. For instance, in the first G5, a classic bluegrass voicing, if you lean your second finger against the fifth string, you can strum all the strings without hearing that string. Compared to Example 1's full fingerings, 5 chords have an edge that works very well for rock (the ubiquitous rock power chord is just roots and fifths), blues, rootsy country, bluegrass, Celtic, or any other style where you want a sound that is neither obviously major nor minor.

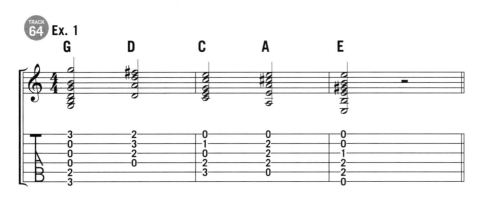

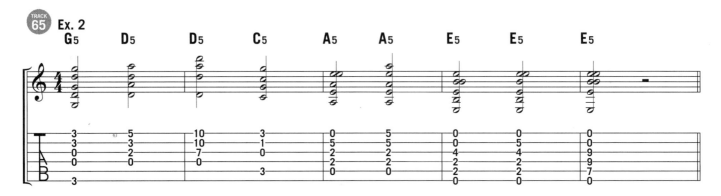

Strum Fewer Strings

Now let's reduce things further, by playing only some of the strings, as in **Example 3**. Take care to play only the strings shown. If you have to skip over a string, as in the first G5 and the first C5, mute the unwanted string with the adjacent fretting finger. These reduced voicings are less familiar to the ear and leave lots of room for the vocal or instrumental melody (and as a bonus, they're easy to grab). Also, if you play, say, a G chord on just the bass strings, you can later switch to the high strings or a full six-string voicing for a dramatic contrast. It's like dynamics: if you play as hard and loud as you can all the time, you have nowhere to go but down; if you withhold some volume and intensity, you can pump up or soften the sound. By playing only some of the notes and strings, you have more options for varying the sound.

Another great way to use these pared-down voicings is to include a bass note other than the root. The fingerings in **Example 4** use either the third or fifth of the chord in the bass below the types of reduced chord voicings shown in Examples 2 and 3. For instance, G5/D has the D (the fifth of a G chord) in the bass; G/B has the B (the third of G) in the bass. As we'll see in subsequent examples, these alternate-bass chords let you create a nice flow in a progression.

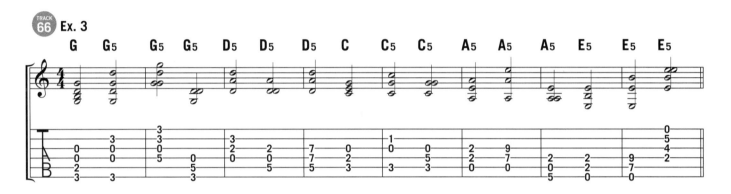

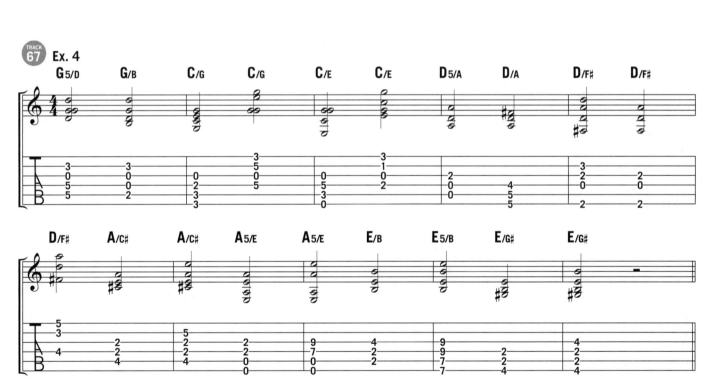

These reduced voicings are less familiar to the ear and leave lots of room for the vocal or instrumental melody (and as a bonus, they're easy to grab).

Put 'Em Together

Let's combine everything we've discussed in a simple progression using G, D, and C chords. **Example 5** is a bassier version of a normal G–D–C–D progression, with alternate bass notes on the D and C (the open third string in the D/A adds a sus flavor, which you can leave out if you want just the basic chord tones). **Example 6** focuses on the middle strings, with one small embellishment added to the C by playing the open second string on the way to the D/F♯. In **Example 7**, the sound is more trebly and deli-

cate. As you can see and hear, the familiar G–D–C–D progression has become a lot more interesting: In addition to some nice bass movement and a smoother flow between chords, we've opened up space for the melody or other instruments (which we can also leave empty for a pared-down sound). These examples are starting to sound more like a song than a generic progression.

Let's see how these ideas work in my original song, **"Humming My Way Back Home,"** a ballad in 6/8 time, in the key of G. It's no accident that this song has reduced chord

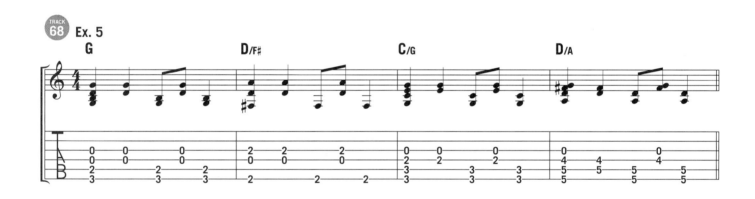

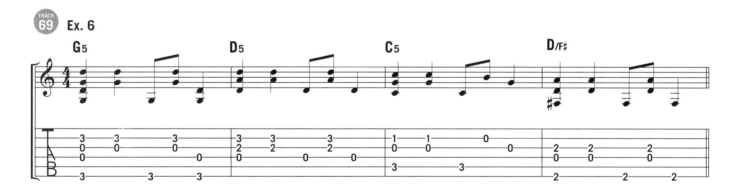

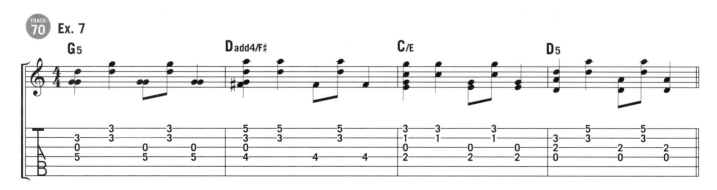

RHYTHM GUITAR ESSENTIALS

voicings—I wrote it on a Strumstick, a guitar-like instrument with only three strings, two of which are tuned an octave apart. (Note that my CD version, which can be heard on MySpace and seen on YouTube, includes Strumstick, guitar, and bass; in this version I'm combining elements of all those parts to create a stand-alone guitar accompaniment.) The song's verses rock back and forth between G and D, and the low roots-and-fifths fingerings allow the melody lots of space to soar above. The chorus also stays mostly on the bass strings until the end, when the contrast created by adding notes on the treble strings matches the sense of resolution in the lyrics. Note the tangy C chord in measure 14, with the F♯ (the sharp fourth of C) and G next to each other—this comes from the original Strumstick part. At the end of the chorus, I hang onto the high G note (first string, third fret) over both the G and D chords to create a more sustained sound. The instrumental bridge moves up and down the neck with power-chord–style voicings—dig into these chords to really bring out the drama.

Have fun with the song, and try out similar voicings in your own repertoire. Remember, the secret of great accompaniment is to give the song just what it needs . . . and no more.

Humming My Way Back Home

Words and music by Jeffrey Pepper Rodgers

Coda

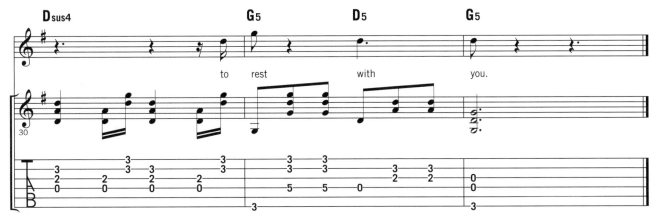

	G5	**D5**
1.	Stand by the window and raise it wide	

G5   **D5**
Open your ear for a song

   G5   **D5**
I'm turnin' the corner and comin' inside

G5   **D5**
Weary but never so strong

Chorus
   Em   **D/F♯**   **G**
I'm humming my way back home

Em   **D/F♯**   **C5(♭5)**   **G5**
Humming my way back home to you

Em   **D/F♯**   **G**   **C**
Humming my way back home, love

   G5   **Dsus4 G5**   **Dsus4**
To rest with you as night rolls through

G5   **D5**
2. Living is longings and lessons half-learned

   G5   **D5**
Our words tangle up in a knot

    G5   **D5**
Let's forget what we've given, forget what we've earned

   G5   **D5**
Give thanks for the love that we've got

Repeat Chorus

	G5	**D5**
3.	Winter is coming, the leaves blow down	

G5   **D5**
Daylight is slipping away

G5   **D5**
Stoke up the fire and gather around

    G5   **D5**
There's no place where I'd rather stay

Repeat Chorus
G5   D5   G5
To rest with you

TACKLING DIFFICULT CHORDS

Jenny Reynolds

Once you progress beyond learning the basic, open-position chords, your fingers may start to find themselves in unfamiliar territory. Physically challenging shapes like barre chords can be daunting for beginners, and other exotic chords may look as though they'd only be playable if you sprouted more fingers. Even some common major and minor chords—like F and Bm—are difficult to play no matter what you do. Don't worry, in this lesson we'll show you how you can make difficult chords easier by learning them in a step-by-step manner—first by getting your fingers in position without putting any pressure on the strings and then alternately fretting and relaxing your fingers so that your muscles "learn" the new chord.

Read from Your Diagram

With most material for new guitarists, chord names are accompanied by diagrams that tell you exactly where each finger should go on the fretboard. The following diagrams illustrate common ways to make F and Bm chords—two chords that beginners encounter fairly early on and often find difficult to play. Even the most explicit diagram can lead to confusion if you don't know how to read it, so if you're already scratching your head, consult the Music Notation Key.

Without pressing down on the strings, try forming these two chord shapes on the neck of your guitar. Position your barred index finger first and then add your other fingers according to the numbers at the top of the diagram. The X's in the diagram show you which strings not to pick.

Posture-Perfect Position

If these chords give you trouble, it's a good idea to think about your arm position and posture. If you're tilting your fretboard

> *If you're tilting your fretboard upward so you can see what your fingers are doing, it will be more difficult to play these chords clearly.*

upward so you can see what your fingers are doing, it will be more difficult to play these chords clearly, and you could even be inviting wrist injury down the road. Instead, sit up straight and position the guitar so that you're looking at the top edge of the fretboard, with the waist of the guitar flat against your leg. Keep your fretting arm from resting on your leg so that you can bend your wrist easily. If you're used to playing while hunched over the fretboard, this new posture-perfect position may feel a bit unnatural at first, but you'll find it will pay serious dividends when it comes time to dig into difficult chord shapes.

Make Sure Every Note Sounds

To see what I mean, go ahead and try the F chord. Without pressing down, barre the tip of your index finger on the first fret, against just the top two strings, as shown in the photo. Bring your left elbow in toward your torso. Next, move your middle finger to its place on the third string (second fret), put your ring finger on the third fret of the fourth string, and keep your pinky slightly raised so that it doesn't touch your other fingers or any of the strings. Compare your fingering with the diagram.

When you think you have it, press down and strum. You're only playing four strings here, but you want to make sure they all sound, so try picking the strings one at a time, as in **Example 1**. If one note doesn't sound, it could be that one of your other fingers is touching the string, interfering with the vibration. If a note sounds buzzy, check to make sure that each of your fingers is positioned directly behind the fret, and try again (and again) until you find the right sound.

Strum and Relax: Drill That Shape!

Once you've got the F chord down, you want your fingers to "remember" that shape. Help it stay lodged in your muscle memory by playing the shape repeatedly (**Example 2**), loosening your fingers between each strum without taking them off the strings. Strumming and relaxing in this way helps your

fingers remember their positions relative to each other. Next, try alternating it with another familiar chord, like the F–C progression in **Example 3**.

Now let's try a couple of new chords. The jazzy Fmaj7 chord in **Example 4** has a shape like an Am but with an F on the sixth string. Beginning with your first finger, place your fingers in sequence on the strings without pressing down on the fretboard. When they're all in place, press down and strum. As before, try playing this shape a few times, making sure to relax your fingers between each strum. As you do this, pay attention to the sound the chord makes, so you train your ear and fingers at the same time.

Do the same thing with the chord in **Example 5**, a Bm7♭5 (pronounced B-minor seven flat five)—a chord you're definitely not likely to see in instructional materials for beginners. Nonetheless, this chord has a distinctive sound and a movable

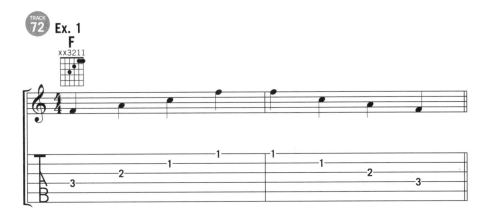

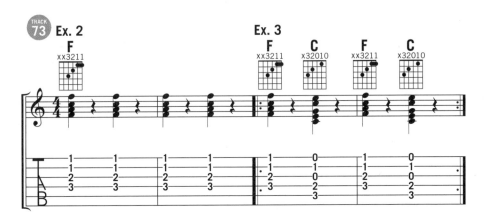

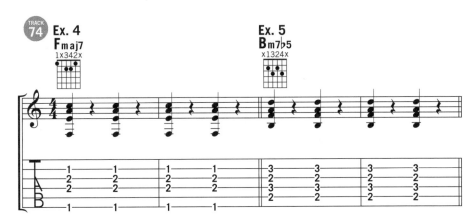

shape (meaning that you can move it up and down the neck to form other chords), both of which make it useful. Once you feel comfortable with Examples 4 and 5, try **Example 6**, which should help you really lock in both of these chord shapes.

For more practice with these chords, try **"Summer Twilight Blue,"** which uses some chords you probably already know, like D7, as well as the Fmaj7 and Bm7♭5 chords you just learned. Before you play the song through, take a moment to scan through the music and familiarize yourself with any new

chord shapes you see. Get to know them using the same steps outlined above, and practice switching between chords that fall next to one another in the music. If the eighth-note arpeggios are too much to deal with right away, just strum the chords in a smooth, quarter-note pattern.

Even if you feel comfortable with a wide variety of chords, there will come a day when you'll run into a piece of music with a chord you don't know. By approaching new chords in this methodical manner, you'll be playing the changes in no time.

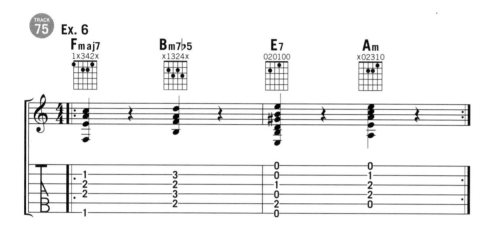

Summer Twilight Blue

Music by Jenny Reynolds

OPEN-STRING CHORDS

Wayne Riker

By combining open-string notes with fretted notes, you can transform mundane chords into colorful new voicings, some of which include pitch combinations that are otherwise physically impossible to play. These new chordal possibilities can add harmonic depth to your songwriting repertoire, inspire fresh new second-guitar parts, and allow you to create fuller solo-guitar arrangements. But the best thing about the chords you'll learn in this lesson is that you already know how to play them.

The easiest way to create open-string chords is to take some of your favorite shapes and leave out a few notes, substituting open strings for fretted ones. We'll start by looking at an Am chord played at the eighth fret. Leave out the root note (A) on the second string and the third (C) on the first string, and you get an Am with an added ninth—Am(add9). The ninth is the open second string (B).

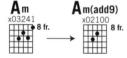

Next, start with a Dm shape in fifth position and delete the A note at the fifth fret on the top string. The open E string produces a ninth, and you've got a Dm(add9) chord.

Play **Example 1**, a simple i–v minor chord pattern, to see how these two chords sound together. Use a basic strum to help your ear warm to the harmonic depth and color of these

The easiest way to create open-string chords is to take your favorite shapes and leave out a few notes, substituting open strings for fretted ones.

voicings. Then try different strumming and fingerpicking patterns to create your own rhythmic nuances.

Move Chord Shapes up the Neck

Another way to create open-string chords is to slide first-position shapes up the neck, adding open strings on top of, or in between, fretted notes. (For the most common shapes, see "Instant Open-String Chords.") By moving a root-position F triad two frets higher and playing the open high E string, you get a G6 chord.

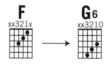

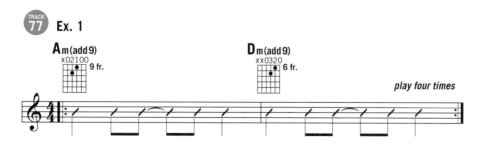

INSTANT OPEN-STRING CHORDS

Sliding shapes you already know up the neck creates great-sounding chords. Move the following open-position chords up the neck to each designated fret location. Use the lowest fretted note in each chord as a fret reference.

Move the C chord to frets three (Dadd4/add9), six (Fmaj9), eight (G6), and 11 (B♭6♭5).

Move the D chord to frets four (E/D), five (Dm7), seven (G/D), nine (A/D), ten (B♭/D), and 12 (D9sus4).

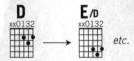

Move the E chord to frets three (F#11), four (G6), six (Aadd9), eight (Badd4), nine (Cmaj7), and 11 (D6/9).

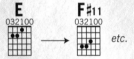

Move the Am chord to frets three (Bm11/A), five (Amaj7), six (Dm[add9]/A), eight (Em/A), and ten (A6).

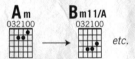

You can also try moving an open-position B7 chord to frets four (D13), six (E7), eight (F#11), and 11 (A9) or an open-position C7 chord to frets three (D9), eight (G13), ten (A7), and 12 (B11).

Slide an A5 power chord up three frets to form a C5 power chord, add the open B and E strings, and you have a Cmaj7 chord.

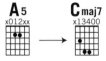

You can also try this with chord inversions. Slide an F/C chord up to sixth position and let the open E string ring, and you get a B♭ chord with an alluring flatted fifth.

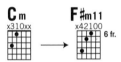

Example 2 is a sweeter way to voice a I–IV–♭VII–♭III progression using these chords and an Fmaj9 (measure 3) formed by sliding a C chord up to the sixth fret. Although this example sounds cool with the rolling arpeggio picking pattern shown, experiment with different strum and fingerpicking patterns.

Now let's take a few simple triads and see what we get when we move them up the neck. Move a root-position C-minor triad up to sixth position and add the open B and E strings and you create an F#m11 chord.

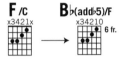

Slide a Baug triad up one fret and add the open E and B strings and you have a C#7#5(#9) chord.

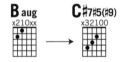

Ex. 2 (TRACK 78)

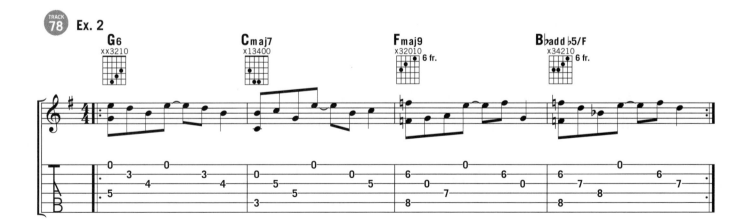

Example 3 shows how these two chords sound in a minor-key i–V7 progression.

Barre Chords Without the Barre

You can also create some nice open-string chords by taking barre-chord shapes and removing some or all of the barre, letting the open strings ring through. Let's start with the fifth-position A barre chord. Free up the top two strings from the barre and the open B string becomes the ninth of an Aadd9 chord.

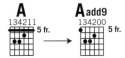

Example 4 uses this chord in a I–IV progression with a D6(9) chord that is formed by sliding a C triad up two frets.

If you remove the barre from a fifth-position A7 chord, add the open A string, and leave your index finger on the fourth string, an A9 chord is born.

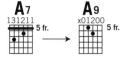

If you take a B7 barre-chord form and remove the barred first string, you get a B7add4 chord. But let's take this one step further: Remove your pinky from the second string and you create a spicy B7sus4.

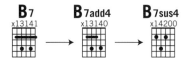

TRACK 79 Ex. 3

TRACK 80 Ex. 4

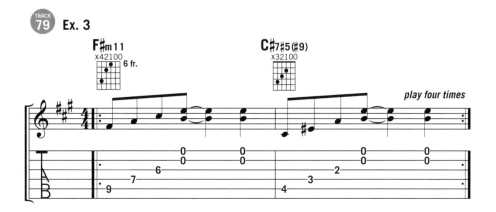

TRACK 81 Ex. 5

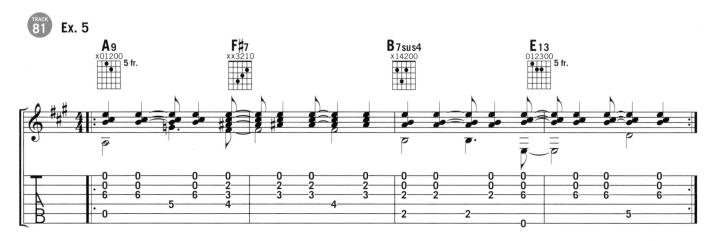

Example 5 shows a slick way of using these chord voicings through a I7–VI7–II7–V7 progression in the key of A. Note the F♯7 chord in bar 2 (an F triad moved up two frets).

Let's finish by playing some of these chords in a song—**"The Aftermath**." You'll see a few new chords here, so let's quickly look at each one. The Em9 chord in bar 1 and the G13♭9 chord in bar 10 are embellished open-position chords. The Am(add9) voicing in the first bar and D13 chord in bar 3 are built from fifth-fret Am and D9 barre chords, respectively. The Am9 in bar 19 is formed by moving an open-position Bm7 chord up to the 12th fret and adding the open high E string.

The D6(9) in bar 9, Fmaj9 in bar 16, and Em(add9) in the final bar are all built around C-shape chords slid up the neck, while the F♯7 in bar 5 is a simple F triad slid up one fret.

I use a hybrid pick-and-fingers technique to play "The Aftermath." This enables me to fingerpick using my pick and middle and ring fingers while keeping a flatpick in hand for the single-note runs and strummed chords.

This lesson should give you just a taste of the kinds of open-string chords you can create. Try to find some of your own using the approaches I've described.

The Aftermath

Music by Wayne Riker

RHYTHM GUITAR ESSENTIALS

AUGMENT YOUR CHORD KNOWLEDGE

David Hodge

Believe it or not, there's more to life than major and minor chords. Oh yes, there are sevenths and add9s and even 13ths of different sorts. But at the core, those are just fancy major and minor chords, and many players seldom venture beyond those two basic chord types. Indeed, many guitarists don't even know there are not two but four families of chords. In addition to major and minor, there are also the augmented and diminished chords. If the terms sound exotic, rest easy: They are relatively easy to learn and play. What's more, they can add quite a bit of pizzazz to your playing and songwriting style.

Augmented Chords

All four basic chord types are built on the same scale degrees, taken straight from the major scale. The difference lies in whether or how we make changes in those notes. Major chords are formed using the root, third, and fifth. A C-major chord, for example, has the notes C (the root), E (the third) and G (the fifth). Lower the third a half step and you get a minor chord—so Cm is C, E♭, and G.

If you start with your major chord and raise the fifth by a half step, you'll get an augmented chord (sometimes designated by a "+" symbol in chord sheets). Using C as an example again, you would make a C-augmented chord by playing C, E, and G♯.

Play **Example 1** and listen to the differences between a C and Caug chord in open position. You can hear that the augmented chord sounds transitional—it definitely wants to take your ears to another chord. In fact, augmented chords are usually followed by IV or minor VI chords (F and Am, respectively, in the key of C), as demonstrated in **Example 2**.

An interesting thing to notice is that each note of the augmented chord is the interval of a major third (two steps, or four frets) apart from the next. This means that when you learn one augmented chord, you've actually learned three. The notes of Eaug, for example, are E, G♯, and B♯ (which is the same note as C), while the notes of G♯aug are G♯, B♯ (C again) and D♯♯ (which is E). This fact alone can save you a lot of trouble in learning new chords!

Adding a seventh to an augmented chord is a favorite substitution of jazz and blues players. **Example 3** shows a typical V–IV–I–V turnaround, using Gaug7 instead of the usual G7 one might play. This particular fingering is a movable chord, meaning that you can use it up and down the fingerboard in order to play various augmented-seventh chords.

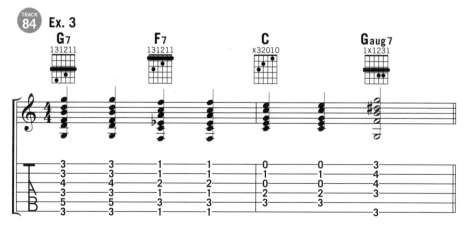

Diminished and Diminished-Seventh Chords

Diminished chords, sometimes denoted by the degree symbol (°), are made by lowering both the third and the fifth of the major chord. Going back to the key of C, Cdim would contain C, E♭, and G♭. Here the notes are a minor third (a step and a half, or three frets) apart. Because a guitar's standard tuning is in fourths, it's difficult to play many diminished chords in open position. More often than not, you'll find yourself simply picking out the proper notes—as in **Example 4**, which is our Cdim chord once again. To give your ears a great demonstration of the difference between major chords and diminished chords, try using open-position D chords, as shown in **Example 5**.

The chances of your running into diminished chords are fairly rare, but you will quite frequently find diminished-seventh chords popping up. To make a diminished-seventh chord, start with your diminished chord and add the sixth to the pile. Cdim7, demonstrated in **Example 6**, consists of C, E♭, G♭, and A.

When you see a diminished-seventh chord on a chord chart, your first reaction may be to panic. But, unlike diminished chords, dim7 chords are easy to find and play on the guitar. Take a look again at Example 6 and notice the shape. If you can remember this shape and can find the root note of your diminished-seventh chord anywhere on the first four strings, you're set for life. And the bonus here, as with the augmented chord, is that one diminished seventh chord is actually four chords! Cdim7 has the same notes as E♭dim7, G♭dim7, and Adim7. **Example 7** gives you all the possible diminished-seventh chords, all within the first three frets.

Another cool thing about these chords is that you can shift them up the neck with ease. In **Example 8**, we take our Cdim7 from Example 6 and slide the entire shape up the fingerboard, three frets at a time. Diminished sevenths provide you with an easy, yet very dramatic-sounding, transition from one section of the fretboard to another.

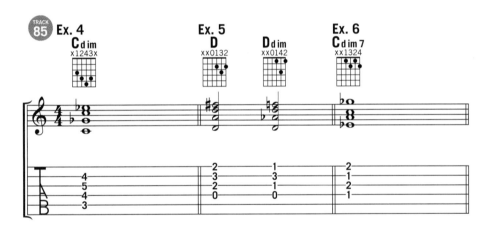

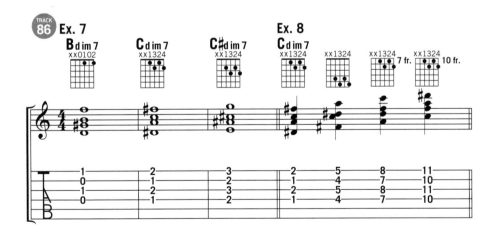

RHYTHM GUITAR ESSENTIALS

Make the Mundane More Interesting

The true fun of both augmented and diminished-seventh chords comes when you realize that you can drop one or two of them into almost any song. As noted earlier, augmented chords are great substitutes for dominant-seventh chords, and diminished-seventh chords can liven up almost any standard chord progression you know. Let's take a typical I–IV–V progression: **Example 9** starts with a C–F–G sequence and, by adding the Caug and F#dim7 chords to it, we give it a jazzy, almost ragtime, feel. Likewise, the C–Dm–G progression of **Example 10** gets a big lift from the C#dim and Gaug7. In this example, we create C#dim by keeping the E and G of the C chord in place and simply raising the C root note up to C#. Not only is it easy, but it gives you a great walking-bass line.

Let's take some of these ideas to create a jazzy arrangement of the old standard "**Frankie and Johnny**." Vamp between C and Cdim in the first three measures, then use Caug in measure 4 to set up an F/Caug7 vamp in measures 5 and 6. We'll go all out for the song's final line, adding Adim7 in measure 7, a chromatic walk from C#dim to Cdim in measure 8, and a nice walking-bass line from G to Adim7 in measure 9. Finally, Gaug7 will bring us back to our original C/Cdim vamp.

Play around with these new chords. The more you get used to them, the more places you'll probably hear them in the songs you listen to. And you'll also find lots of ways to use them, not only in the songs you already know, but also in the songs you write. Augmented and diminished chords can help you create both catchy melodies and arresting harmonies in your own songs.

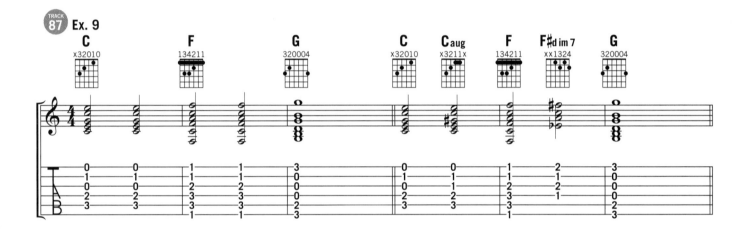

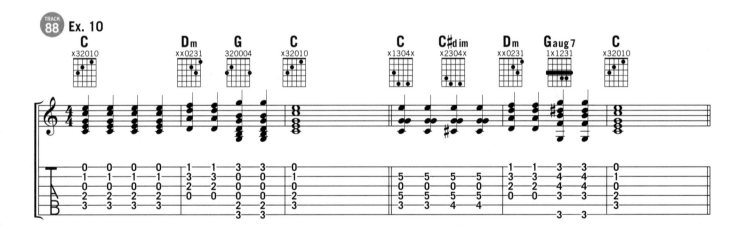

Frankie and Johnny

Traditional, arranged by David Hodge

1. Frank-ie and John-ny were lov-ers   Lord-y how they could love   They
2. *See additional lyrics.*

swore to be true to each oth-er   just as true as the stars a-bove he was her

man   but he done her wrong

C	**Cdim**	**C**	**Cdim**

1. Frankie and Johnny were lovers

C   **Cdim**   **C**   **Cdim**
Lordy how they could love

F   **Caug**   **F**   **Caug**
They swore to be true to each other

F   **Adim7**   **C**
Just as true to the stars above

C#dim C#dim G   **Gaug7**   **C**   **Cdim C Cdim**
He was her man but he done her wrong

C	**Cdim**	**C**	**Cdim**

2. Frankie she was a good woman

C   **Cdim**   **C**   **Cdim**
And Johnny was a good man

F   **Caug**   **F**   **Caug**
And every dollar that she made

F   **Adim7**   **C**
Went right into Johnny's hand

C#dim C#dim G   **Gaug7**   **C**   **Cdim C Cdim**
He was her man but he done her wrong

RHYTHM GUITAR ESSENTIALS

HENDRIX-STYLE EMBELLISHMENTS

Karen Hogg

As one of the most influential guitarists of all time, Jimi Hendrix made an impact on many forms of music. Even if you don't listen to him, you've almost certainly listened to someone who admires Hendrix and his musical legacy. Artists as varied as late blues legend Stevie Ray Vaughan, jazz guitarist Tuck Andress, and classical great Benjamin Verdery have all covered Hendrix songs. Of course, most people think of Hendrix as an incendiary electric guitarist. So what, you may ask, as an acoustic player, do I have to learn from him? The answer is: plenty. In this lesson, we'll explore Jimi Hendrix the rhythm guitarist. We'll delve into some of the facets of his style that made his rhythm playing so influential and talk about how you can apply these concepts to your own playing.

Cool Chord Choices

Hendrix's style developed from a blend of influences—soul, R&B, rock, blues, and jazz—and he honed his chops as a session guitarist for acts such as Little Richard, Sam Cooke, and the Isley Brothers before breaking out on his own. One of the most interesting components of Hendrix's style was his choice of chords. He regularly employed chords with nonchord tones added. In fact, one of Hendrix's favorite chords, the sharp-nine

chord (from "Purple Haze" and other songs), is informally known as "the Hendrix chord." This chord adds the sharp nine (♯9) to the dominant seventh chord (1, 3, 5, ♭7). For instance, the notes in an E7♯9 chord are E, G♯, B, D, and G. Check out the rhythm part in **Example 1**, which contains both the D7♯9 and A7♯9 chords. Keep in mind that it can sometimes be difficult to voice a five-note chord on the guitar—the fifth is left out in both of these voicings.

Hendrix also liked the sound of suspended chords, especially the sus2. To voice a suspended chord, take out (or suspend) the third of the chord and replace it with either the

Jimi Hendrix's style developed from a blend of influences— soul, R&B, rock, blues, and jazz.

 Ex. 1

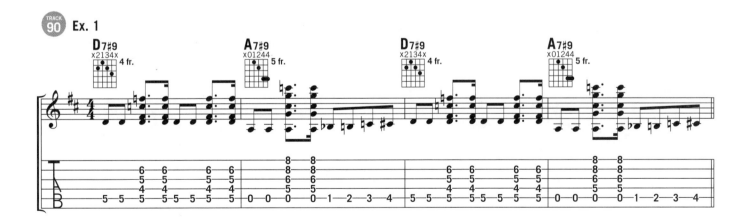

second (sus2) or fourth (sus4). A Dsus2 chord contains the notes D, E, and A; a Dsus4 contains D, G, and A. **Example 2** uses Csus4, Fsus2, and Gsus2 chords.

Thumb the Bass

Hendrix had fairly large hands and would often use his thumb to grab the bass notes of chords. In **Example 3** use your thumb to play the bass notes in each chord. While most of the chords here could be played without the thumb, using the thumb makes it much easier to play progressions like this, which is probably why Hendrix used his thumb so much. Also notice the chromatic movement of the chords in the second measure, another technique Hendrix often employed (either with full chords or bass notes). In this example, the progression moves back to the A chord. Those of you with smaller hands might have difficulty with this one, so if it hurts, don't

do it. ("No pain, no gain" doesn't apply here.) You can finger the chords normally or leave out the bass notes and just play the voicings on the upper strings.

Embellish It

One of the main elements of Hendrix's rhythm style was his chordal embellishment. Check out songs like "Little Wing" and "Wait Until Tomorrow" for examples of this. Hendrix rarely, if ever, simply strummed chords. The Jimi Hendrix Experience was a trio, which left him a lot of room to breathe as a guitarist, so he used slides, hammer-ons, and pull-offs, among other things, to create lush, full arrangements. If you're a solo performer, studying Hendrix's style can help you find ways to fill out arrangements of your own tunes.

Example 4 is a simple progression in the key of E major, with no embellishments. These barre-chord voicings are just

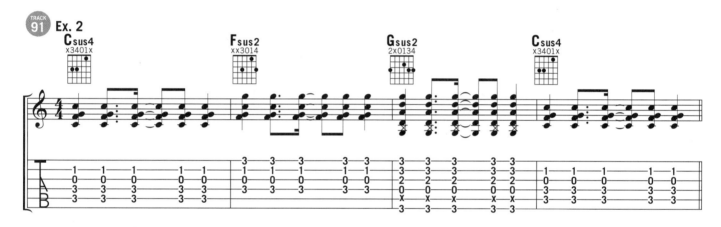

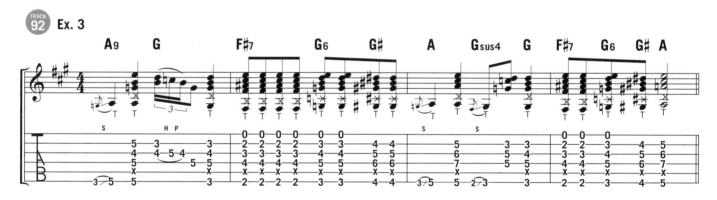

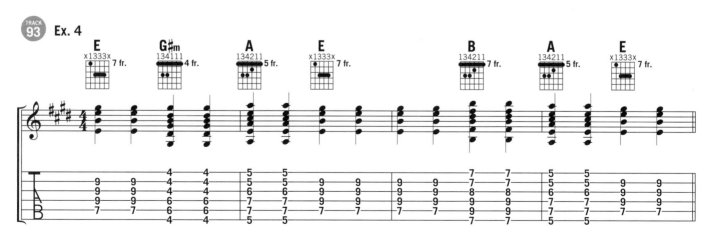

RHYTHM GUITAR ESSENTIALS

one example of how you could play these chords, but they give you a good sense of the progression. **Example 5** spices up this progression a bit with some hammer-ons and partial chords. There are a couple of things to note in this example. First, the chord voicings don't just stick to one area of the neck. Hendrix made use of the entire fretboard in his rhythm playing, and learning chord voicings all over the neck is an important step in developing your rhythm chops. Second, full chords are rarely used here. Hendrix often used these small, two- or three-note voicings. When you play two notes, that interval can imply a chord. For instance, take the C♯ and E notes at the beginning of the second measure. C♯ is the third and E is the fifth of an A major chord. The only note that's missing is A. Therefore, when you play the C♯ and E together, it's going to sound like an A chord (or a C♯m chord, depending on what your bass player is playing). If you're playing on your own, your ear will tend to fill in the missing A note after you've played this progression a few times.

Example 6 uses pull-offs to embellish the same chord progression. This example and Example 7 also use nonchord tones (notes not in the chord). For instance, at the beginning of

Example 6, you play an E and a C♯ note. C♯ is not part of the E chord, but it is immediately pulled off to a B, which is the fifth of E. These nonchord tones help create a fuller sound and serve as passing tones from one chord tone to the next. To finger the A chord in measure 2, barre your index finger across the second fret of the first four strings and use your pinky to play the fifth fret of the first string and your middle finger for the pull-off from the D to the C♯ on the second string. For the E chord in that measure, keep your index finger barred and move your pinky to the fifth fret of the second string and your ring finger to the fourth fret of the third string. To play the lick in measure 4, use your ring finger on the seventh fret of the fifth string, pinky on the seventh fret of the fourth string, and middle finger for the sixth fret of the third string. Stretch your index finger to the fourth fret of the third string for the pull-off.

Slides can inspire further embellishments (**Example 7**) and provide a feeling of movement and fluidity within a chord progression. Notice the sliding double-stops used for the A and B chords (use your index finger for these slides). Hendrix liked this technique, often sliding two notes or even a whole chord shape. The intro to "Castles Made of Sand" is a classic

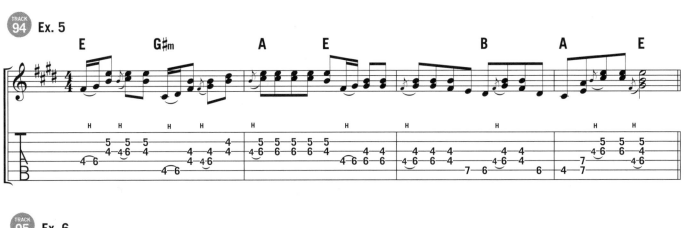

example of this. **Example 8** uses a lot of sliding chord shapes, this time with a different chord progression.

The next example (**Example 9**) integrates some of the techniques we've discussed so far, including hammer-ons, pull-offs, and slides. **Example 10** gives you more practice with these techniques on a different chord progression and adds some bass notes played with the thumb and a sliding chord shape in the second measure. Some of these techniques might be a little difficult at first, but with a little practice, you'll master them. Practice them slowly and make sure all the notes ring out clearly and sustain as long as possible.

When applying these techniques to your own playing, you don't have to play this way through the entire song, as Hendrix sometimes did. Remember, he was in a trio, so he had the

musical space, but if you're in a larger band, you can add hammer-on/pull-off/slide flourishes here and there. The late Curtis Mayfield was great at this type of playing and Hendrix was probably influenced by him at some point. Listen to "People Get Ready" (recorded with the Impressions, Mayfield's 1960s band). After the first verse, he plays some beautiful chordal embellishments that lead nicely to the next verse.

The music in this lesson gives you an introduction to Jimi Hendrix's style, but obviously, there is much, much more to this legendary guitarist. To get more familiar with his style, check out some of his CDs, like *Are You Experienced?*, *Axis: Bold as Love* (my favorite), *Electric Ladyland*, and *Band of Gypsys*. Listen, learn, and enjoy!

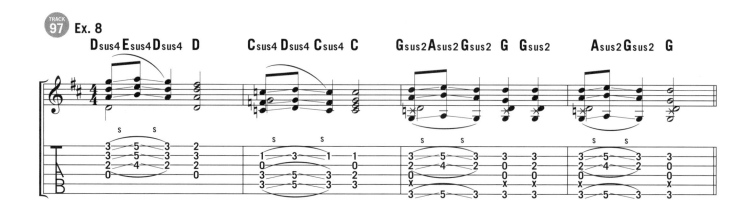

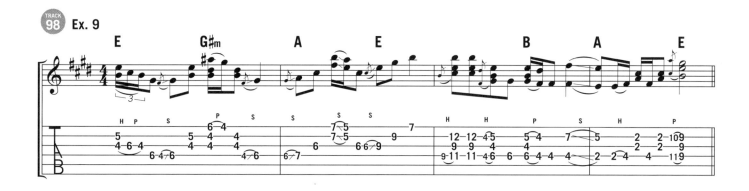

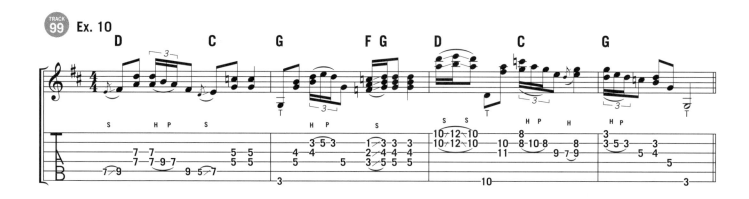

ABOUT THE TEACHERS

ANDREW DUBROCK

Andrew DuBrock transcribes, edits, and engraves music for print and multimedia publications. His clients include *Acoustic Guitar*, Homespun, Solid Air Records, and independent musicians like Alex de Grassi and Michelle Shocked. DuBrock was *Acoustic Guitar's* music editor from 1999 to 2007. He missed the gang so much that he pestered them until they parked his name on the masthead as a contributing editor. DuBrock lives in Portland, Oregon, with his wife and daughter.

CHRIS GRAMPP

Chris Grampp has been playing a wide range of guitar styles, including jazz, swing, blues, and rock, for 35 years. He studied with Tuck Andress, Howard Roberts, and George Barnes and leads his own eclectic band, Club Sandwich. Grampp has taught at the California Coast Music Camp, the Puget Sound Guitar Workshop, and the Sound Acoustic Music Camp and has led workshops at numerous festivals, including the Strawberry Music Festival and the Sonoma County Folk Festival.

DAVID HAMBURGER

Acoustic Guitar contributing editor David Hamburger (www.davidhamburger.com) is the author of more than a dozen books, including *Acoustic Guitar Slide Basics*, *The Acoustic Guitar Method*, *Early Jazz and Swing Songs for Guitar*, and *The Acoustic Guitar Fingerstyle Method*. His fingerstyle, slide, and electric-blues instructional videos are available at www.truefire.com. Hamburger produced Austin, Texas, songwriter Michael Fracasso's CD *Red Dog Blues*, scored the Kestrel Filmworks documentary *Wildcatting for Wind*, and fathered an heir named Milo, all without his head exploding—yet. Hamburger has been playing folk and blues music since first picking up the guitar at the age of 12 and has been on the faculty of the National Guitar Workshop since 1988. His guitar, slide guitar, and Dobro playing can be heard on his solo albums *King of the Brooklyn Delta* (Chester, 1994) and *Indigo Rose* (Chester, 1999), as well as numerous independent recordings. He lives in Austin, Texas.

DAVID HODGE

David Hodge has for years provided backup to numerous Berkshire County, Massachusetts, singer-songwriters. But teaching music is his first love. In addition to his private students, he teaches group guitar lessons for the Berkshire Community College. And guitar students of all ages and levels from more than 168 countries read his lessons at Guitar Noise (www.guitarnoise.com). He is the author of *The Complete Idiot's Guide to Playing Bass Guitar* (Alpha Books).

KAREN HOGG

Karen Hogg is a multi-instrumentalist, music teacher, freelance writer, and yoga instructor living in Nashville. She is the author of two instructional books, *Women in Rock* and *Guitar Made Easy*. Her writing has appeared in *Acoustic Guitar, Guitar Teacher, Play Guitar!, Fretboard Journal*, and *All About Jazz New York*. When not involved in the previously mentioned pursuits, she can be found at various music stores in Nashville, playing guitars that cost more than her annual income.

JENNY REYNOLDS

Jenny Reynolds (www.jennyreynolds.com) is a singer-songwriter and guitar teacher who has taught at the Kerrville Folk Festival and the National Guitar Workshop. A formidable fingerpicker, she loves showing others how to improve their right-hand work. Her own music has been featured on major network television. She has three nationally released CDs and has recorded with Ruthie Foster, Ian McLagan, Catie Curtis, and Duke Levine. A native New Englander, Reynolds now lives in Austin, Texas. She was hailed as the Best New Local Act in the *Austin Chronicle's* 2005 Critics Poll, but she does not own cowboy boots yet.

WAYNE RIKER

Wayne Riker (waynerikerguitar.com) is a freelance guitarist, author, and guitar instructor currently teaching in San Diego, California. He has written seven instruction books, including *Mastering Blues Guitar* and *Blues Licks Encyclopedia*, and produced two instructional DVDs for Alfred Publishing. Riker has been on the faculty of the National Guitar Workshop since 1989, taught group seminars throughout the country, and contributed instructional articles to *Guitar Player* and *Acoustic Musician*. He has played thousands of gigs in nearly every musical setting. On his days off Riker keeps a low profile at home in coastal Carlsbad, California, enjoying red wine and the Pacific Ocean breezes.

JEFFREY PEPPER RODGERS

Jeffrey Pepper Rodgers (www.jeffreypepperrodgers.com) is the founding editor of *Acoustic Guitar* magazine and author of *Rock Troubadours* (a collection of conversations with Paul Simon, Jerry Garcia, Joni Mitchell, and more) and *The Complete Singer-Songwriter: A Troubadour's Guide to Writing, Performing, Recording, and Business*. Rodgers' song "Fly," from his solo CD *Humming My Way Back Home*, won a grand prize in the John Lennon Songwriting Contest. He lives outside Syracuse, New York, where he writes and edits for *Acoustic Guitar*, reports on the music scene for NPR's *All Things Considered*, and hosts the Words and Mus ic Songwriter Showcase.

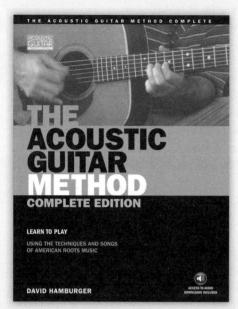